The Natural Pet Food COOKBOOK

by
Wendy Nan Rees
with
Kevin Schlanger, DVM

Illustrations by
Troy Cummings

HEALTHFUL RECIPES
FOR DOGS AND CATS

BICENTENNIAL
1807
WILEY
2007
BICENTENNIAL

Wiley Publishing, Inc.

Library of Congress Cataloging-in-Publication Data:
Rees, Wendy Nan.
  The natural pet food cookbook : healthful recipes for dogs and cats / Wendy Nan Rees, with Kevin Schlanger ; illustrations by Troy Cummings.
     p. cm.
  Includes index.
  ISBN-13: 978-0-470-22530-1
  ISBN-10: 0-470-22530-0
  1. Dogs—Food—Recipes. 2. Cats—Food—Recipes. I. Schlanger, Kevin. II. Title.
     SF427.4.R43 2008
     636.7'085—dc22
                       2007034339

Printed in the United States of America

10 9 8 7 6 5 4 3 2 1

Book design by LeAndra Hosier and Kathie Rickard
Cover design by Troy Cummings
Book production by Wiley Publishing, Inc. Composition Services

Table of Contents

From Wendy: Dedicated with love to Carol Ann Blinken Emquies, my beautiful and talented sister, for inspiring me to keep following my dreams and for always being there for me with her wholehearted love and support. And to my sister Natasha Stanton, without whose pushing me never to give up on my writing and love for pets, this book would not have happened. To both of my wonderful sisters, I say thank you; this one is for you both!

From Dr. Kevin: This book is dedicated to my wife, Suzanne; my children, Nicky, Aviva, Orly, and Michaela; and my dogs, Sydney and Sulley. They all make it easier for me to help treat animals in need.

Acknowledgments

In writing this book, I have been blessed to work with some amazing people, without whom I could not have done this project. I would like to thank Ruthie Bently, the owner and consultant of Bently's Beasties, with a background in canine and feline nutrition, for all the time and unconditional love she offered me. Without her organizational and typing skills, I could not have met my deadlines. To Mary Disney, thank you, you are my guardian angel and an amazing rock of support. Your constant smile and positive attitude brighten every day. To Dr. Kevin Schlanger, thank you for taking the time to help me write this book and for always being ready to be a guest on my radio show. I could not have written this cookbook without your help, time, and patience. To Larry Turner of Larry Turner and Associates, who has been with me since the beginning; your dry sense of humor and ability to remain calm in any situation have continuously led me in the right direction. To Freddie Goldberg, thank you for all the e-mails and phone calls and for calming me down on those few very stressful days. To Pam Mourouzis, the best editor I have ever had, thank you so very much for believing in me and always being there. To my friends and family, you know who you are. Thank you for helping me through this summer with your friendship, love, and humor when the going got tough! I can always count on you making me laugh and helping me get focused. To Anabella, Luca, and Nico Emquies, Tata wants to say thank you for my beach days and all the love you have given me all the time; next time don't tell me the water is not cold! I love you forever and a day! To my grandmother, Ruth Koch, thank you; you are an inspiration at 88! To Hank and Molly, thank you; what a ride—nice to see where we are going! To my mom and dad, thank you, and I love you! And last but not least, to my three boys, Senny, Cappy, and Little Man, thank you for all your taste testing and sitting by my side for 16 hours some days, when we all know your bedtime is 8PM. I love you three so very much! I was blessed the day each of you came into my life! BARK ON!

Foreword

We are all familiar with the adage "You are what you eat." Well, imagine how much more applicable that would be if we ate the same thing every day. That is the case with our four-legged companions. All of their nutrition comes from the food that we provide for them, and that puts a tremendous responsibility on us to ensure that their diet meets their every need. In addition, if the nutrients we supply are not sufficiently healthy, or even not appealing to them, well, they simply will not eat. As a veterinarian, I often have to answer difficult questions regarding complex behavioral changes, such as pets getting into the garbage or, worse, eating inedible objects. Very often these behaviors can be linked to diets that are poor in nutritional value or deficient of certain vitamins or minerals.

In my practice, we will rarely address even the most simple medical conditions without discussing diet. Whether it is a minor skin condition or a complicated metabolic disorder, changes in diet are always part of the treatment plan. In this day and age, while there are many prescription diets to choose from, most are not designed to meet the individual taste buds or personality of every pet. For this reason, having simple recipes that are both nutritious and appealing is a great way to supplement your pet's diet and help give him a happier and longer life.

It is important to stress that these recipes are designed to be supplemental and are not replacements for everyday food. While cooking for your animal companion can be a very rewarding, and sometimes bonding, experience, our pets have different physiological needs than we do. In fact, even different breeds have different nutritional requirements and may tolerate certain foods differently. For example, Bulldogs and Boxers require a specific proportion of fiber in their diets, or they will be more prone to stomach irritations and diarrhea. Before embarking on an entirely home-cooked feeding regimen for your pet, you must have him thoroughly examined by a veterinarian to determine his exact needs. If your pet is older or has a history of recurring illness, certain diagnostics, including full bloodwork, may help determine what type of diet best suits his individual needs.

Always remember that healthy pets help make happy pets. What better way to keep your pets healthy than by feeding them a healthy diet?

—Kevin Schlanger, DVM

About the Authors

Wendy Nan Rees has been involved in the pet industry for more than 25 years, starting when she founded Lip Smackers, Inc., dedicated to providing healthy, all-natural treats for dogs. The Lip Smackers bakery still operates out of the Pet Care Company in Hermosa Beach, California. Wendy created so many recipes that she was inspired to write her first book, *No Barking at the Table: Canine Recipes Most Begged For*. The book was so well received that *No Barking at the Table 2* and *No Catnapping in the Kitchen* followed. Wendy then published *The Name Game*, a collection of celebrity essays on how and why they named their pets, along with over 1,000 suggestions of pet names.

Wendy's success as an author and dog treat creator led to numerous TV appearances. She was the Pet Lifestyle Advisor on Animal Planet's *Petsburgh, USA*, and has appeared on the Home Shopping Network. She also wrote a monthly column called "In the Kitchen with Wendy" for *Your Pet Magazine*.

Not one to rest on her successes, Wendy then helped to create Cedar Green, a line of all-natural pet odor eliminators. The signature product is Freshen Vac, a heat-activated odor eliminator that can be used in vacuum cleaners, dog beds, and air vents.

In 2000, Wendy was diagnosed with breast cancer, which forced her to take a break from her career to focus her energy on her recovery. Today, she is happy to be cancer free and working on her Internet radio show, *Wendy's Animal Talk*, which airs Tuesdays at 1PM PST at www.healthylife.net. She also writes the colum "Two Minute Dog Advice" for www.lovetoknow.com Her new line of natural pet products can be found on her website, www.wendynanrees.com.

Wendy lives in Los Angeles with her dogs Senator, Cappy, and Little Man.

Kevin Schlanger, DVM, is the owner of Westside Animal Medical Associates and chief veterinarian of Brent-Air Animal Hospital, located in Los Angeles. After a successful career as a management consultant for Price Waterhouse and the New Jersey Transit Corporation, he decided that his true calling was caring for animals. He was accepted to the top veterinary school in the country, the University of California, Davis—a notable achievement for an out-of-state applicant. During his four years there, he received numerous awards and scholarships, including the prestigious Payday Luff Memorial Scholarship for excellence in oncology and infectious disease and the Theodora Peigh Scholarship for demonstrated contributions in international programs. He graduated with honors in June 2000.

Dr. Schlanger first worked as an associate at an animal hospital in West LA. In 2003, he took over the practice at Brent-Air Animal Hospital. In two short years, what was a small one-doctor practice became a bustling three-doctor practice complete with boarding and grooming facilities. Dr. Schlanger quickly became one of the most sought-after veterinarians in Los Angeles, and Brent-Air Animal Hospital is now one of its most respected facilities. Nutrition is one of Dr. Schlanger's areas of expertise. In addition, he gives back to the community by working with nonprofit rescue groups such as Best Friends Animal Society and Westside German Shepherd Rescue.

Dr. Schlanger and his wife, Suzanne, are the proud parents of four children, Nicky, Aviva, Orly, and Michaela, as well as two dogs, Sydney, a Cocker Spaniel, and Sulley, a Cavalier King Charles Spaniel.

Introduction

In the late 1960s and early '70s, organic and all-natural foods were becoming commonplace in human diets. As we became more aware of what we were putting into our own bodies, it seemed only natural that we began to consider what we were feeding our pets.

Little did I know that my first job, at the young age of 17, would shape the course of my life. My duties included taking care of the Goldstein family's two girls and working four days a week at their Katonah, New York, store Lick Your Chops, one of the very first all-natural pet stores. Robert Goldstein was and still is a prominent veterinarian, now based in Westport, Connecticut. After 30 years in the holistic pet industry, Goldstein and his wife, Susan, remain pioneers in the field. Their book *The Goldsteins' Wellness and Longevity* has won numerous awards.

What I learned in that summer of '78 was the reason I started cooking for my pets. In 1985, I welcomed home my first puppy, a Chinese Shar-Pei. Six weeks later, he became very ill. Weeks of tests showed that he was allergic to soy, salt, and preservatives. At the time I was in cooking school and newly married, but I thought, how hard could it be to create some food or at least a treat for my dog? To my surprise, learning the ins and outs took about 8 months; just figuring out how to make the treats crunchy without burning them was a challenge. Lip Smackers®, the people cookie made for dogs, was born, and so was my career in the pet industry.

After graduating from cooking school, I started the company Lip Smackers and began applying everything I had learned while I worked for the Goldsteins. For example, they taught me that brewer's yeast is wonderful for dogs; it helps bitter the blood to retard fleas. Since writing my first cookbook in 1991, I have been on a mission to teach people how to cook and care for their pets in a healthy, all-natural way, always keeping it easy, fun, safe, and practical.

In 2007, for the first time we had a major pet food recall. This recall turned the industry upside down. Having lost confidence in pet food manufacturers, more and more pet parents are looking for healthy recipes that they can cook for their dogs and cats—like the recipes I have been creating since 1985. This book contains all-new, all-natural recipes.

I have had the good fortune to work closely on this book with Kevin Schlanger, DVM, who is my own pets' veterinarian. In addition to providing tips for you, Dr. Kevin has reviewed all the recipes in this book to make sure that they are safe for your pets.

Adding Home-Cooked Meals to Your Pet's Diet

When considering home cooking for your pets, it is very important that you consult your pet's veterinarian—just as you would consult your doctor before changing your own diet. Even though I have written this book with Dr. Kevin, we can't stress enough that every dog and cat is different. Always err on the side of caution and safety.

Even after the pet food recall, I haven't completely taken my pets off their regular kibble. Some commercially made foods are very good for pets, containing the correct amounts of vitamins, minerals, and nutrients. I mix commercial kibble with homemade kibble and supplement with loaves, soups, stews, and casseroles. Each pet also gets a multivitamin every day. If you are thinking of putting your pet on an entirely homemade diet, you must learn about a dog's or cat's specific nutritional and caloric needs and resting energy requirements (also known as RER). Please seek the help of a veterinary medical professional.

When making changes to your pet's diet, you must do so gradually, allowing his digestive system time to adjust. I suggest that you take about 2 weeks for the process so that your pet is less likely to have stomach upset or diarrhea.

- **Days 1–4:** Feed 75% of the old food and 25% of the new food.
- **Days 5–8:** Feed 50% each of old and new food.
- **Days 9–12:** Feed 25% of the old food and 75% of the new food.
- **Day 13 and on:** Feed all new food.

If your pet has allergies, it is especially important to check with your veterinarian before cooking for your furry friend. Note that all the recipes in this book allow for substitutions. For example, if your dog is allergic to wheat, you can try rice flour instead.

Information for Dog Owners

How Much to Feed Your Dog

When explaining to your veterinarian that you would like to begin feeding some home-cooked meals, make sure to discuss portion size. The serving sizes in this book are based on a medium-sized adult dog who weighs 25 to 35 pounds. Your vet will be able to help you determine the appropriate portion size for your pet, especially if your pet has weight issues or is very small or large. It is important to take into account your pet's age, activity level, metabolism, and other health issues.

Although every dog's needs are different, here are some general guidelines for how much to feed a healthy adult dog. Remember, 1 cup = 8 ounces.

Feeding Chart for Dry Food (Kibble)

Weight of Dog	Amount Per Day
0–5 lbs	Up to 3/4 cup
5–10 lbs	3/4 cup–1 1/4 cups
10–20 lbs	1 1/4 cups–2 cups
20–40 lbs	2 cups–3 1/3 cups
40–60 lbs	3 1/3 cups–4 2/3 cups
60–80 lbs	4 2/3 cups–5 3/4 cups
80–100 lbs	5 3/4 cups–6 3/4 cups

Feeding Chart for Wet Food
(Loaves, Soups, Stews, and Casseroles)

Weight of Dog	Amount Per Day
0–5 lbs	3/4 cup–1 1/3 cups
5–14 lbs	1 1/3 cups–2 2/3 cups
14–35 lbs	2 2/3 cups–5 1/3 cups
35–50 lbs	4 cups
50–75 lbs	7 cups
75–100 lbs	8 cups

Once you know that your pet can tolerate and do well on homemade foods, start weighing your pet. I suggest keeping track for about 6 months. If he stays in the same healthy weight range, you know you're doing a good job.

The Nutrients a Dog Needs

Nutrients are important to all living things, and dogs are no exception. Dogs are omnivores—they eat not only meat, but also grains, grasses, and other foods. They will even scavenge if they have to.

Proteins provide nutrients to a dog's organs, muscles, connective tissues, and bones. A diet lacking in protein can affect your dog's immune system. Proteins are comprised of twenty-three amino acids. The ten amino acids that a dog's body can't manufacture, called essentials, must come from his daily diet. When cooking for your dog, make sure to use a variety of proteins, such as lean beef, chicken, turkey, lamb, duck, and even fish.

Carbohydrates provide energy and fiber. Some carbohydrates, like rice, are also good sources of protein. In your dog's meals, use rice, pasta, oats (usually in the form of rolled oats), wheat berries, bulgur, barley, rye, or millet.

Just like children, most dogs need to acquire a taste for **vegetables and fruits.** I like to use canned plain pumpkin because it offers many vitamins and fiber, is low in calories, and is naturally sweet. Other vegetables to try include alfalfa sprouts, asparagus, broccoli, carrots, corn, green beans, peas, yellow squash, and zucchini.

The average dog should eat at least three ½ cup servings of vegetables and one ½ cup serving of fruit a day. To make sure that my dogs are getting theirs, I give them frozen vegetable/fruit purée. Here's my basic recipe: Put the following ingredients in a blender or food processor: 4 ounces no-salt-added Italian plum tomatoes, drained; 1 cup cooked drained chopped spinach; ½ cup plain pumpkin; ½ cup cooked chopped green beans, drained; ½ cup unsweetened applesauce; ¼ cup blueberries; ¼ cup mashed bananas; and ½ cup baby carrots. Blend to a purée, pour into ice cube trays, and freeze. Once frozen (about 24 hours), remove from the ice cube trays and store in zippered plastic bags for up to 3 months.

Healthy **fats** provide energy and vitamins. Fats can also affect whether your dog has a shiny coat. They are important for the health of your dog's eyes and brain, for blood clotting, and for reproduction. Soluble fats provide a dog with vitamins A, D, E, and K. Fish oil is the best source of fat you can give your dog. Choose high-quality vegetable oil, safflower oil, corn oil, sesame oil (great flavor in small amounts), wheat germ oil, sunflower oil, flaxseed oil (an excellent source of omega-3 fatty acids), or olive oil. Even cod liver oil a couple times a week is great for a dog's coat. Note that cod liver oil, wheat germ oil, and flaxseed oil must be refrigerated, as they can turn rancid if not kept cold.

Vitamins and minerals are the building blocks of any healthy organism, your dog included.

- **Vitamin A** is used for fat absorption and is necessary for a healthy, shiny coat; normal growth rate; good eyesight; and reproduction.
- **Vitamin B** protects the nervous system. It's also necessary for a dog's coat, skin, growth, and vision.
- **Vitamin C** is synthesized in a dog's liver. It is added to foods because, although dogs can manufacture some vitamin C in their bodies, they can't manufacture their daily requirement.
- **Vitamin D** promotes healthy bones and teeth.
- **Vitamin E** helps with proper functioning of muscles and internal reproductive organs.
- **Vitamin K** helps with blood clotting.
- **Calcium and phosphorus** must be given in the correct ratio to protect bones.
- **Copper** helps with strong bones and prevents anemia.
- **Iodine** prevents goiter in dogs, the same way it does in people.
- **Iron** provides healthy blood and protects against fatigue and anemia.
- **Magnesium** helps protect against convulsions.

- **Potassium** helps with a healthy nervous system.
- **Zinc** helps with normal growth and healthy skin and coat.

Commercial pet food manufacturers add vitamins and minerals to dry and canned pet foods to ensure a balanced diet. Although the meals in this book are healthy and well-balanced, make sure to add a vitamin/mineral supplement (choose one specially formulated for dogs, made of natural whole-food ingredients, and containing no preservatives or artificial ingredients) to make the meal nutritionally complete. Your vet can help you determine the proper vitamins and minerals to give to your dog in supplement form. Never add a supplement before or during the cooking process, or when food is still hot, as doing so will deteriorate its benefits.

Information for Cat Owners

How Much to Feed Your Cat

Although every cat's needs are different, here are some general guidelines for how much to feed a healthy adult cat. If you have a kitten, a lactating queen, an overweight cat, or an older cat, her nutritional needs will be different; please consult your veterinarian. Remember, 1 cup = 8 ounces.

Feeding Chart for Dry Food (Kibble)

Weight of Cat	Amount Per Day
0–5 lbs	Up to 1/2 cup
5–10 lbs	1/2 cup–2/3 cup
10–15 lbs	2/3 cup–1 cup

Feeding Chart for Wet Food
(Loaves, Soups, Stews, and Casseroles)

Weight of Cat	Amount Per Day
0–4 lbs	3 ounces–3 3/4 ounces
5–8 lbs	5 1/4 ounces–7 1/2 ounces
9–12 lbs	8 ounces–11 1/4 ounces
13–16 lbs	10 1/2 ounces–15 ounces
17–22 lbs	15 ounces–20 1/4 ounces

The Nutrients a Cat Needs

In nature, cats make their own choices when it comes to meeting their nutritional needs, but we must make those choices for our domesticated cats. Cats are carnivores; those in the wild eat 90% protein and 10% carbohydrates and greens.

A cat's dietary needs are very different from a dog's, and a cat will not do well on a diet made for dogs. Cats need wet food because 70% of their water intake comes from wet food. Cats also need more protein and fat than a dog might. Felines require certain vitamins, like retinol and niacin, and certain amino acids, such as taurine, daily. Taurine, found only in animal tissue, is essential for good eyesight.

Protein, which is made up of amino acid chains, is the backbone of all growth and tissue repair in a cat. Cats need a high-protein diet, as protein is their primary source of energy. Protein is also used in the processes of circulation and kidney function and to maintain the support structure of the cat's body (tendons, bones, muscles, and ligaments). The best sources of digestible protein for cats are chicken, beef, fish, eggs, and dairy products like cottage cheese and yogurt.

Cats don't have the same need for **carbohydrates** as dogs because they get a lot of the calories they need from other sources. This doesn't mean that you have to stop feeding carbohydrates; your cat just may not need as many.

Since a cat's diet consists mainly of protein, fat, and water, **vegetables and fruits** are not as necessary as they are for dogs. However, they are good sources of vitamins, minerals, and fiber. Fiber helps keep a cat regular and prevents hairballs, which, if not taken care of, can cause an intestinal blockage. Therefore, fruits and vegetables can be added to your cat's daily diet and will only benefit your pet.

Fats are the most concentrated source of energy for your cat. Fat is an excellent source of linoleic and arachidonic acids, which are essential for a healthy skin and coat. Fat also provides vitamins A, D, E, and K. Cats' livers metabolize fat for energy. What fat the body doesn't use is stored or released through urine. A cat with a fat deficiency will not grow well and will have dandruff and dry hair. She may become listless and can be more susceptible to disease or infection.

A cat's vitamin and mineral needs, while basically the same as a dog's, can be more challenging to meet. Here is a list of the vitamins and minerals that are essential to a cat's good health:

- **Vitamin A** is used by the eyes, reproductive organs, and skin.
- **Vitamin B:** As there are several B vitamins, I have listed them separately. Vitamin B-12 and niacin are used for the functions of enzymes in the body. Pantothenic acid is used to metabolize energy. Riboflavin is used for the functions of enzymes in the body. Thiamine (vitamin B-1) is used for energy and to metabolize carbohydrates.
- **Vitamin D** helps maintain mineral status, phosphorus balance, and skeletal structure.
- **Vitamin E** defends against oxidation damage.
- **Vitamin K** helps with blood clotting, bone protein, and other proteins.
- **Folic acid** is used to metabolize amino acids and helps synthesize protein.

- **Calcium** is used in the formation of bones and teeth, muscle contraction, transmission of nerve impulses, and blood clotting.
- **Chlorine** helps with the acid/base balance in the body.
- **Copper** helps the body metabolize iron and form blood cells and connective tissues.
- **Iodine** aids in thyroid hormone utilization, growth and development, and metabolic rate regulation.
- **Iron** helps with metabolizing energy and utilizing hemoglobin and myaglobin.
- **Magnesium** assists with the structure of bones and teeth, is used in enzyme functions, and helps with hormone secretion and function.
- **Manganese** aids in neurological and enzyme functions and the development of bones.
- **Phosphorus** assists with DNA and RNA structures, locomotion, and metabolism of energy and balances the acid/base ratio.
- **Potassium** helps with transmitting nerve impulses and enzyme reactions.
- **Selenium** helps the body's immune response and defends against oxidation.
- **Sodium** helps balance the acid/base ratio and helps with the generation and transmission of nerve impulses.
- **Zinc** promotes healthy skin, healing of wounds, and utilization of proteins and carbohydrates.

Commercial pet food manufacturers add vitamins and minerals to dry and canned foods to ensure a balanced diet. Although the meals in this book are healthy and well-balanced, make sure to add a vitamin/mineral supplement (choose one specially formulated for cats, made of natural whole-food ingredients, and containing no preservatives or artificial ingredients) to make the meal nutritionally complete. Your vet can help you determine the proper vitamins and minerals to give to your cat in supplement form. Never add a supplement before or during the cooking process, or when food is still hot.

Tools of the Trade: Kitchen Equipment Needed

This section contains a quick list of the pots, pans, and utensils you will need to make the recipes in this book.

- Baking pan, 9-x-13-inch
- Blender or food processor
- Casserole dishes, 8-inch and 12-inch
- Cheese grater
- Colander
- Cookie sheets (I use 18-x-13-inch)
- Cutting board, plastic
- Ice cube trays or Popsicle molds

- Knives
- Loaf pan
- Long-handled heavy-duty spoon
- Measuring cups, liquid and dry
- Measuring spoons
- Mixer
- Mixing bowls, stainless-steel
- Pastry brush
- Ring mold, large

- Roasting pan, 9-x-13-inch
- Rolling pin
- Saucepan, 4-quart, with lid
- Skillet, 10- to 12-inch
- Spatulas, rubber and slotted
- Stockpot, 8-quart or larger, with lid
- Vegetable peeler
- Whisk
- Wooden spoon

The Pet-Friendly Pantry

It is helpful to have some staple ingredients on hand that can be used in a variety of recipes. Here is a list of the basic items I like to keep in the pantry or freezer so that I can prepare meals for my pets at a moment's notice:

- Active dry yeast
- Baking soda (bicarbonate of soda)
- Beans, dried
- Beef broth or stock, low-sodium or no-salt
- Bone meal (human-grade)
- Bread crumbs, plain dry
- Brewer's yeast
- Chicken broth or stock, low-sodium or no-salt
- Cornmeal (yellow or white)
- Cornstarch
- Dried fish flakes
- Eggs, large
- Flour, all-purpose (or plain) and quick-mixing
- Freeze-dried fruits and vegetables
- Milk powder, nonfat
- Gelatin, unflavored

- Molasses (treacle)
- Parmesan cheese
- Parsley (or parsley flakes)
- Pasta
- Peanut butter (for giving a pill)
- Pineapple, canned crushed
- Pumpkin, canned plain
- Rice, brown and white
- Rolled oats
- Salt (or salt substitute)
- Spinach, frozen chopped
- Sweet potatoes
- Tuna, dark packed in oil
- Thai fish sauce
- Wheat germ, plain (not honey-flavored)
- Worcestershire sauce

Note: Just like humans, dogs and cats need a small amount of salt each day to protect them against dehydration and maintain normal bodily functions. Although fresh foods contain natural sodium, they may not contain enough to meet the animal's daily requirement. Even commercial pet food companies add salt to their foods. For that reason, I call for salt—either sodium chloride (table salt) or potassium chloride (salt substitute)—in some recipes. Consult your veterinarian if your pet has a special health issue, such as kidney or heart problems, that may mandate a limited salt intake. Potassium chloride provides essential nutrients without the possible challenges of table salt, so if you are uncomfortable feeding table salt, feel free to substitute potassium chloride.

If a recipe does not specify a certain form of an ingredient (such as fresh, frozen, or canned), or your market doesn't carry a specific item, feel free to use whichever form you have on hand. Choose whole foods and fresh ingredients whenever possible, and opt for the low- or no-salt varieties of canned foods. I suggest using organic or all-natural ingredients when you can buy them for a reasonable price. Be careful about offering leftovers from your own meals, which may be too spicy for your pet's system to handle.

Foods to Avoid Feeding Your Dog or Cat

Dogs and cats enjoy a variety of proteins, fruits, vegetables, and carbohydrates, but certain foods can be toxic to pets. It is very important that you follow this "Do Not Feed" list closely:

- Alcoholic beverages
- Artificial sweeteners—NutraSweet, sorbitol, Sweet'N Low, xylitol, and so on
- Avocado
- Candy
- Chocolate (all forms)
- Coffee (all forms)
- Fatty foods
- Garlic
- Grapes
- Macadamia nuts
- Moldy or spoiled foods
- Mushrooms
- Onions and onion powder
- Raisins
- Salt
- Seeds of any type
- Yeast dough

When in doubt about the safety of a particular food, call your vet, or call the ASPCA Poison Control Hotline at 888-426-4435.

Cooking and Storing Foods in Bulk

I get many e-mails from radio listeners telling me that they are cooking for their pets two or three times a week and it is becoming a burden. I suggest setting aside 2 days a month for cooking; with proper storage and freezing you'll be in good shape. Almost all of the recipes in this book are very simple, and two or three can be made in a day. I like to set aside 1 or 2 days a month for making stews or loaves and then freeze them so that I have a month's worth of food prepared. For example, I will take one Sunday a month and make one large stew recipe and one loaf recipe, so I'm using the oven and the stockpot or slow cooker at the same time. I store a week's worth of food in the refrigerator and freeze the rest. That way, I can alternate between stews and loaves from the freezer, my pets don't have to eat the same thing meal after meal, and I'm not cooking every day.

I have also discovered a vacuum-sealed food storage system called Seal-A-Meal, which makes freezing and storing a breeze. If you are going to purchase a few things for cooking for your pets, I suggest purchasing one of these.

Conversion Tables

Liquid Measures

American	Imperial	American	Imperial
1/4 cup	4 tablespoons	1 1/2 cups	1/2 pint + 4 tablespoons
1/3 cup	5 tablespoons	2 cups	3/4 pint
1/2 cup	8 tablespoons	2 1/2 cups	1 pint
2/3 cup	1/4 pint	3 cups	1 1/2 pints
3/4 cup	1/4 pint + 2 tablespoons	4 cups	1 1/2 pints + 4 tablespoons
1 cup	1/4 pint + 6 tablespoons	5 cups	2 pints
1 1/4 cups	1/2 pint		

Solid Measures

American	Imperial	American	Imperial	American	Imperial
Butter		**Flour**		**Sugar**	
1 tablespoon	1/2 ounce	1/4 cup	1 1/4 ounces	1/4 cup	1 3/4 ounces
1/4 cup	2 ounces	1/2 cup	2 1/2 ounces	1/2 cup	3 ounces
1/2 cup	4 ounces	1 cup	5 ounces	1 cup	6 1/2 ounces
1 cup	8 ounces	1 1/2 cups	7 1/2 ounces	**Vegetables**	
Cheese (grated)		2 cups	10 ounces	1/2 cup	2 ounces
1/2 cup	2 ounces	**Herbs**		1 cup	4 ounces
Cornmeal		1/4 cup	1/4 ounce	**Wheat Germ**	
1 cup	6 ounces			1/2 cup	1 1/2 ounces
				1 cup	3 ounces

Oven Temperatures

Degrees Fahrenheit	Gas Mark	Degrees Celsius	Degrees Fahrenheit	Gas Mark	Degrees Celsius
225–250	1/4–1/2	110–120	375	4	180
250–275	1/2–1	120–140	400	5–6	190–200
275–300	1–2	140–150	425–450	7–8	220–230
300–350	2–3	150–160	450–475	8–9	230–240

Part I: *Dogs*

1

Kibbles and Casseroles

KIBBLE MAY SEEM BORING, BUT FEEDING YOUR DOG KIBBLE IS IMPORTANT. CHEWING HARD, CRUNCHY FOODS HELPS CLEAN TEETH AND PREVENTS TARTAR BUILDUP AND GINGIVITIS, WHEREAS WET FOOD TENDS TO SIT BETWEEN TEETH. YOU DON'T WANT TO OMIT KIBBLE FROM YOUR DOG'S DIET.

MAKING HOMEMADE KIBBLE MAY SOUND DIFFICULT, BUT ONCE YOU'VE TRIED THESE RECIPES, YOU WILL SEE THAT IT'S NOT DIFFICULT AT ALL. THE MAIN THING TO REMEMBER ABOUT MAKING YOUR OWN KIBBLE IS THAT YOU NEED TO LET IT DRY OUT IN THE OVEN IN ORDER TO REMOVE THE MOISTURE AND MAKE THE KIBBLE CRUNCHY. THE DRIER THE KIBBLE BECOMES, THE MORE INTENSE THE FLAVOR IS AND THE LESS CHANCE THERE IS FOR SPOILAGE. HAVING AN 18-x-13-INCH COOKIE SHEET, USUALLY FOUND AT COOKING SUPPLY STORES, MAKES THE PROCESS EASIER, SINCE YOU CAN FIT ALL THE KIBBLE ON ONE SHEET. YOU CAN ALSO USE A LARGE PIZZA PAN WITH HOLES IN THE BOTTOM.

I LOVE CASSEROLES BECAUSE THEY ARE EASILY FILLED WITH HEALTHY INGREDIENTS, THEY WILL KEEP IN THE REFRIGERATOR FOR UP TO 5 DAYS, AND THEY FREEZE BEAUTIFULLY. I TAKE SINGLE-SERVING PORTIONS, SEAL THEM IN VACUUM-SEALED FOOD STORAGE BAGS, AND STORE THEM IN THE FREEZER. WHEN IT COMES TIME TO DEFROST, I SIMPLY PUT A PORTION IN THE FRIDGE THE NIGHT BEFORE, AND WHEN READY TO SERVE I PLACE THE BAG IN WARM WATER TO BRING THE MEAL TO ROOM TEMPERATURE. YOU DO NOT WANT TO MICROWAVE YOUR PET'S FOOD. IT CAN BECOME WAY TOO HOT FOR THEM, AND IT DESTROYS SOME OF THE VITAMINS AND MINERALS YOU HAVE WORKED SO HARD TO INCLUDE.

Kaptin's Krunchy Kibble

𑑛 Makes 20 to 30 servings 𑑛

This is my basic kibble recipe. I keep the first 8 cups in a sealed container in the refrigerator and freeze the rest in vacuum-sealed food storage bags. With the vacuum-sealed food storage system, you can take out only what you need and then reseal the bag. The kibble will keep in an airtight container for 2 weeks in the refrigerator or 3 months in the freezer.

4 cups whole wheat flour

2 cups rye flour

2 cups nonfat milk powder

2 teaspoons bone meal

1 cup plain wheat germ

½ cup chopped fresh parsley, or 2⅔ tablespoons parsley flakes

1 teaspoon kosher salt

4 eggs

1 cup safflower, olive, or corn oil

4 tablespoons Worcestershire sauce

3 cups water

4 cups cooked ground beef, pork, lamb, duck, chicken, or turkey

2 cups cooked and puréed sweet potatoes

1½ cups chopped dried apples

2 cups frozen chopped spinach, thawed and drained

1. Preheat the oven to 300 degrees. Spray two large cookie sheets with nonstick cooking spray.

2. In a large mixing bowl, combine the flours, milk powder, bone meal, wheat germ, parsley, and salt.

3. Beat the eggs and blend them with the oil in a smaller mixing bowl. Add the Worcestershire sauce.

4. Add the water to the flour mixture and mix well.

5. Fold in the egg mixture and combine it all evenly.

6. Add the meat, sweet potatoes, dried apples, and spinach and press them into the dough.

7. Spread the dough on the cookie sheets, making it very flat and thin. Use a knife to cut it into small squares.

8. Bake for 45 minutes to 1 hour or until the kibble is golden brown and not doughy when you break a piece open. During the baking process, take a wooden spoon or spatula and move the kibble around on the cookie sheet so that it bakes evenly. Then turn off your oven, keeping the door closed, and let it dry out in the off oven for at least 4 to 6 hours or overnight.

9. When you remove your kibble from the oven, it will still be slightly warm and moist. Let it sit on cooling racks for another hour or two until it is completely dry and cool.

Variations: Here are some other ingredients I like to add for flavor and nutrients: alfalfa leaf, barley, basil leaf, beets, broccoli, brown rice, carrots, flaxseed meal, green beans, kamut, nutritional yeast flakes, peas, potatoes, rolled oats, rosemary leaf, and zucchini.

Pumpkin and Veggie Kibble

⋙ Makes 20 to 30 servings ⋙

Pumpkin is one of my boys' favorite veggies, and I have the late Governor to thank. A few years back, while I was working on another cookbook, Governor was my main taste tester. When the book was finished, I took him for his yearly shots and found out that he had put on a few too many pounds. (This is why I now spread the job among friends and family members, and of course my three dogs.) My vet suggested adding plain pumpkin to Govey's meals and offering it as a snack. Pumpkin is loaded with fiber, is low in calories, and has lots of beta carotene and vitamin A. It's also naturally sweet, which dogs love. Within a few months, and with a few extra walks, Govey was back to his regular weight. This kibble will keep for 2 weeks in the refrigerator or 3 months in the freezer in an airtight container.

4 cups whole wheat flour

2 cups rye flour

2 cups nonfat milk powder

½ cup rolled oats

2 teaspoons bone meal

1 cup plain wheat germ

1 teaspoon kosher salt

½ cup chopped fresh parsley, or 2⅔ tablespoons parsley flakes

4 eggs

1 cup safflower, olive, or corn oil

1 cup molasses

4 tablespoons Worcestershire sauce

3 cups water

4 cups ground chicken, cooked and then puréed

2 cups canned pumpkin

2 cups frozen chopped spinach, thawed and drained

1 cup dried apples, crushed

1½ cups dried veggies (a mixture is fine—use what you can find)

1. Preheat the oven to 300 degrees. Spray two large cookie sheets with nonstick cooking spray.

2. In a large mixing bowl, combine the flours, milk powder, rolled oats, bone meal, wheat germ, salt, and parsley.

3. In a smaller mixing bowl, beat the eggs. Blend in the oil, molasses, and Worcestershire sauce.

4. Add the water to the flour mixture and mix well.

5. Fold in the egg mixture and combine it all evenly.

6. Add the chicken, pumpkin, spinach, dried apples, and dried veggies and press into the dough.

7. Spread the dough on the cookie sheets, making it very flat and thin. Use a knife to cut the dough into small squares.

8. Bake for 45 minutes to 1 hour or until the kibble is golden brown and not doughy when you break a piece open. During the baking process, take a wooden spoon or spatula and move the kibble around on the cookie sheet so that it bakes evenly. Then turn off your oven, keeping the door closed, and let it dry out in the off oven for at least 4 to 6 hours or overnight.

9. When you remove your kibble from the oven, it will still be slightly warm and moist. Let it sit on cooling racks for another hour or two until it is completely dry and cool. Once dry, break the kibble into pieces.

DR. KEVIN SAYS

Sweet, easily digestible pumpkin is a great source of insoluble fiber. Adding a tablespoon or two to your pet's food can help minimize gas and diarrhea.

Lamb Kibble

W. Makes 20 to 30 servings W.

In the United States, lamb was originally introduced as a substitute for beef or chicken, often combined with rice, for dogs with allergies. The use of a previously unfed protein is how veterinarians typically determine the presence of a food allergy. Lamb is no longer effective in isolating food allergies in dogs because it is now found in most commercial dog foods. Today we have lamb, fish, duck, sweet potato, and several other interesting foods to choose from when feeding our pets. Here is a homemade lamb kibble recipe that your dog is sure to love! It will keep for 2 weeks in the refrigerator or 3 months in the freezer in an airtight container.

4 cups whole wheat flour
2 cups rye flour
2 cups nonfat milk powder
½ cup rolled oats
2 teaspoons bone meal
1 cup plain wheat germ
1 teaspoon kosher salt
½ cup chopped fresh parsley, or 2⅔ tablespoons parsley flakes
4 eggs
1 cup safflower, olive, or corn oil
4 tablespoons Worcestershire sauce
3 cups water
4 cups ground lamb, cooked and then puréed well
2 cups cooked and puréed sweet potatoes
2 cups frozen chopped spinach, thawed and drained

1. Preheat the oven to 300 degrees. Spary a large baking pan with nonstick cooking spray.

2. In a large mixing bowl, combine the flours, milk powder, rolled oats, bone meal, wheat germ, salt, and parsley.

3. Beat the eggs and blend them with the oil in a smaller mixing bowl. Add the Worcestershire sauce.

4. Add the water to the flour mixture and mix well.

5. Fold in the egg mixture and combine evenly.

6. Add the lamb, sweet potatoes, and spinach and press into the dough.

7. Spread the dough in the baking pan, making it very flat and thin. Use a knife to cut it into small squares.

8. Bake for 45 minutes to 1 hour or until the kibble is golden brown and not doughy when you break a piece open. During the baking process, take a wooden spoon or spatula and move the kibble around on the baking pan so that it bakes evenly. Then turn off the oven, keeping the door closed, and let it dry out in the off oven for at least 4 to 6 hours or overnight.

9. When you remove your kibble from the oven, it will still be slightly warm and moist. Let it sit on cooling racks for another hour or two until it is completely dry and cool. Once dry, break the kibble into pieces.

Kibble Tips

When making homemade kibble, you can roll out the dough if you want to, but I use a big spatula and make it as flat as I can on a very large cookie sheet. Then I use a knife to score it into little squares—or I make fun shapes with very small cookie cutters. Kibble makes a great welcome-home gift for a friend.

Cordon Bleu with a Simple Twist

Makes 8 to 10 servings

When I was in cooking school, Chicken Cordon Bleu was one of our first test recipes, and it always stuck with me. Here is my version for dogs. At holiday time, I find that I have a lot of leftover meat, so this is how I use it. This recipe will keep for 3 days in the refrigerator or 2 months in the freezer.

1 pound baked ham, cooked and ground

1 pound ground chicken (grind leftover cooked chicken or start with fresh ground chicken)

¾ cup sweet potatoes, parboiled and then cubed

¾ cup canned plain pumpkin

1 cup cooked brown rice

1 cup shredded Monterey Jack cheese

½ cup corn

2 tablespoons plain wheat germ

1 tablespoon brewer's yeast

3 tablespoons chopped fresh parsley, or 1 tablespoon parsley flakes

3 eggs, beaten

1¾ cup milk

½ cup Parmesan cheese

1. Preheat the oven to 350 degrees. Spray a ring mold, loaf pan, or baking dish with non-stick cooking spray.

2. In a large mixing bowl, combine the ham, chicken, sweet potatoes, pumpkin, rice, Monterey Jack cheese, corn, wheat germ, brewer's yeast, and parsley.

3. Mix the eggs with the milk and pour over the meat mixture. Sprinkle with Parmesan cheese.

4. Bake for 1 hour or until the Parmesan cheese is melted and golden brown and a knife inserted into the center comes out clean. The casserole should hold its shape without jiggling; the egg and milk mixture bakes everything together almost like a custard. Let cool and serve.

Dr. Kevin Says

Soft cheeses, such as cream cheese, are a great way to help hide pills or other oral medications. Because the soft cheese sticks to the medication, it becomes harder for your pet to separate the pill from the cheese, and he is less likely to spit it out.

Tasty Tuna Casserole

When it comes to tuna, the dog does not come to mind first. But just like cats, many dogs love tuna. Tuna is a great source of protein, B vitamins, omega-3 fatty acids, and several minerals, like potassium, selenium, and magnesium. In Japan, tuna and other fishes are the most popular main source of protein. This casserole will keep for 3 days in the refrigerator or 2 months in the freezer in an airtight container.

8-ounce package uncooked noodles
9-ounce can tuna in oil, drained
¼ cup chopped fresh parsley, or 1⅓ tablespoons parsley flakes
1 tablespoon brewer's yeast
3½ tablespoons butter
3 tablespoons flour
2 to 2½ cups milk
½ cup grated Parmesan cheese

1. Preheat the oven to 350 degrees. Spray an 8-inch casserole dish with nonstick cooking spray.

2. Cook the noodles until tender, following package directions. Drain and place in the casserole dish.

3. Add the drained tuna, parsley, and brewer's yeast and mix slightly.

4. Use the remainder of the ingredients to make a white sauce. In a saucepan over medium heat, melt the butter and then whisk in the flour. Slowly whisk in about ¼ cup of the milk. When the sauce gets thick again, add more milk. Repeat until you have the consistency of a smooth gravy. If you are at a high altitude, you may need the extra ½ cup milk to thin the sauce.

5. Add the Parmesan cheese and stir until the sauce thickens further, but is still pourable.

6. Pour the sauce over the noodles and tuna. Bake for 30 to 40 minutes or until a knife inserted into the center comes out clean. Let cool and serve.

PASTA TIPS

When cooking the pasta for this casserole, be sure to drain it very well. If you have cooked too much pasta for your recipe, you can store the leftovers in the refrigerator for 2 days or freeze them for up to a month.

DR. KEVIN SAYS

When choosing canned tuna, look for tuna packed in oil rather than water. It's moister, tastes better, and will provide your pet with additional healthy fats that are necessary in his diet.

Bandit's Beef Casserole

My good friend and dog trainer, Mary E. Disney (yes, a real Disney, second cousin once removed, as she always replies when asked) has a dog named Bandit who is one of the funniest dogs I know. Bandit is an Australian Sheepdog who doesn't go anywhere without his red bandana. I named this casserole in honor of Mary Disney and her little bandito, who ate this entire casserole in one sitting when Mary tested this recipe. I guess it got his seal of approval. You can store this casserole for 4 days in the refrigerator or 2 months in the freezer in an airtight container.

1 pound lean ground beef, cooked and drained

8-ounce can corn, drained

16-ounce can sliced carrots, drained, or 1 pound fresh carrots, cooked and sliced

8-ounce can condensed tomato soup

1 cup shredded Monterey Jack cheese

¼ cup chopped fresh parsley, or 1⅓ tablespoons parsley flakes

1 tablespoon plain wheat germ

½ teaspoon brewer's yeast

¼ cup grated Parmesan cheese

1. Preheat the oven to 350 degrees. Spray 12-inch casserole dish with nonstick cooking spray.

2. Mix together all the ingredients except for the Parmesan cheese and place in the casserole dish. Sprinkle the Parmesan cheese on top.

3. Bake for approximately 25 minutes or until a knife inserted into the center comes out clean. Let cool and serve.

Most dogs eat twice a day. However, this can vary. Puppies are usually fed three times a day—morning, noon, and night—until they are 6 months old. Some adult dogs are fed only once a day, and others have access to a constant supply of food and can eat whenever they are hungry (known as *free-feeding*). I suggest feeding twice a day. The problem with feeding once a day or free-feeding is that you are not able to monitor what your dog is eating as well. If you feed twice a day, you are less apt to end up with an overweight dog, and because he is eating more often, he is less likely to raid your garbage can out of hunger. I also suggest putting the food bowl down for 20 to 30 minutes and picking it up after that if your dog hasn't eaten. Not only does he get put on a schedule, but he is less apt to become a picky eater.

If possible, serve food and water to your pets in stainless-steel bowls, which are virtually break-proof, dishwasher safe, and easy to keep clean. I am not a fan of glass or ceramic bowls for this simple reason: Glass and ceramic can chip, get into your pet's intestines, and cause a big problem. And plastic bowls can release toxins into food and water that sit in them all day.

Remember, too, that fresh water should be made available to your pet 24 hours a day.

Ham Upside-Down Casserole

While driving across country with my three friends after graduating high school, we spent two wonderful days in Pennsylvania Dutch country, where they have wonderful farmers' markets. I was so taken by the handmade quilts, the fresh flowers and produce, and the foods that were for sale: preserves, dressings, meats, baked goods, and puddings. I had never seen or tasted many of the items before. I loved the Ham Upside-Down Casserole. Here's my version. My boys love ham, so I use leftovers to make this fun recipe and always keep some in the freezer. This casserole can be refrigerated for 4 days or frozen for 3 months in an airtight container.

1½ cups cubed cooked ham
1 cup lima beans, cooked and drained
8-ounce can cream-style corn
1 cup (4 ounces) shredded sharp Cheddar cheese
1 teaspoon Worcestershire sauce
¼ cup chopped fresh parsley, or 1⅓ tablespoons parsley flakes
2 tablespoons butter
⅔ cup flour
⅓ cup cornmeal
2 tablespoons plain wheat germ
1 egg
¼ cup milk
fresh parsley for garnish (optional)

1. Preheat the oven to 400 degrees. Spray an 8-inch casserole dish with nonstick cooking spray.

2. In a large mixing bowl, combine the ham, lima beans, corn, cheese, Worcestershire sauce, and parsley.

3. Turn the mixture into the prepared casserole dish, cover, and bake for 15 minutes.

4. In a smaller mixing bowl, combine the remaining ingredients. Spoon over the hot meat mixture, spreading the batter evenly to the edges.

5. Bake for 20 minutes or until golden brown and cooked through. A knife inserted into the center should come out clean. Let cool, cut into wedges, and invert each wedge onto a plate. If you have fresh parsley on hand, use it for garnish.

HAM LEFTOVERS

When I cook a whole ham, I always freeze the leftover meat and the ham bone. With the bone, you can make many great broths and soups—see Chapter 2 for soup recipes for dogs and Chapter 6 for soup recipes for cats.

2

Stupendous Stews, Savory Soups, and a Growlin' Gravy

• •

STEWS AND SOUPS ARE GREAT RECIPES TO MAKE FOR DOGS—YOU CAN SERVE THEM OVER KIBBLE OR AS MEALS BY THEMSELVES. BETTER YET, YOU CAN TAILOR THEM TO YOUR DOG'S TASTES. A STEW IS SIMPLY THICKER THAN A SOUP—IT WOULD BE EQUIVALENT TO A HOMEMADE CANNED DOG FOOD. SOUPS AND STEWS STORE BEAUTIFULLY FOR UP TO 5 DAYS IN THE REFRIGERATOR OR UP TO 3 MONTHS IN THE FREEZER. I FREEZE THEM IN CONVENIENT SINGLE-SERVING PORTIONS AND FEED THEM TO MY DOGS ALMOST DAILY IN BETWEEN SERVINGS OF MY LOAF RECIPES (SEE CHAPTER 3).

ALTHOUGH THE DIRECTIONS I GIVE ARE FOR COOKING ON THE STOVETOP IN A LARGE STOCKPOT (YOU CAN ALSO USE A DUTCH OVEN), ALL THE RECIPES IN THIS CHAPTER CAN ALSO BE PREPARED IN A SLOW COOKER. USING A SLOW COOKER IS MUCH EASIER—YOU CAN SET IT AND GO, AND THE MEAT WILL BECOME VERY TENDER. SET YOUR SLOW COOKER ON HIGH, ADD THE OIL, AND LET IT HEAT UP. THEN ADD THE MEAT OR VEGETABLES. IF YOU ARE BOTH BROWNING MEAT AND SAUTÉING VEGGIES, BROWN THE MEAT FIRST, REMOVE IT, LEAVING THE DRIPPINGS IN THE BOTTOM, AND THEN SAUTÉ THE VEGETABLES IN THE LEFTOVER FAT, WHICH WILL GIVE THEM GREAT FLAVOR. IF YOU HAVE A LOT OF FAT LEFT OVER AFTER THAT, DRAIN THE FAT AND THEN ADD THE NEXT INGREDIENTS. ONCE EVERYTHING HAS BEEN ADDED, BRING IT ALL TO A BOIL, COVER, SET THE SLOW COOKER TO LOW, AND FOLLOW YOUR SLOW COOKER'S GUIDELINES FOR COOKING A STEW; COOKING TIME IS GENERALLY 4 TO 6 HOURS. MANY SLOW COOKERS HAVE A TIMER THAT AUTOMATICALLY SHUTS OFF AFTER THE SET COOKING TIME AND KEEPS THE MEAL AT A CONSTANT, STABLE 170 DEGREES. THIS STOPS THE COOKING PROCESS BUT KEEPS THE MEAL FRESH AND WARM. I USE A SLOW COOKER ALL THE TIME WHEN COOKING FOR MY DOGS.

Little Man's Stew

〰 Makes 8 servings 〰

I like to cook this stew on top of the stove—it makes the house smell wonderful. I serve it over kibble. Freeze it in ice cube trays for up to 3 months so that you have single servings that you can pop out of the freezer and reheat. The stew can be refrigerated for 1 week. If you are not feeding your dog kibble, you can serve this stew alone.

1 tablespoon olive oil

1 pound beef, duck, lamb, chicken, or turkey, cubed

2 sweet potatoes, peeled and cubed

1 cup uncooked pasta, any shape (I like to use vegetable pasta)

½ cup dry lentils

1 cup chopped green beans

1 cup corn

1 cup peas

½ cup uncooked brown rice

8 to 10 cups vegetable, beef, or chicken broth (depending on desired consistency)

½ cup chopped fresh parsley, or 2⅔ tablespoons parsley flakes

1 tablespoon yellow cornmeal mixed with 2 tablespoons cold water

1. In a large stockpot, heat the olive oil over medium-high heat. Add the meat and brown well on all sides.

2. Add the remaining ingredients except for the cornmeal mixture. Bring to a boil, cover, and simmer for up to 2½ hours. Depending on what type of meat you've chosen, it may be ready in as little as 1½ hours—just check that the meat is cooked through and the sweet potatoes and pasta are soft.

3. To thicken the stew, stir in the cornmeal mixture and bring it back up to a boil for 3 to 4 minutes. Remove from heat, let cool, and serve.

Ruthie's Chompin' Chicken and Turkey Stew

⚘ Makes 8 servings ⚘

Ruthie Bently has been my wonderful assistant for the past few years. It is terrific to have Ruthie in Minnesota and me in Los Angeles, because whenever I am testing a new recipe, Ruthie also tests the recipe up in Minnesota, where the altitude and climate are completely different. Sometimes we even find that different ingredients are available at her supermarket. Ruthie's chicken and turkey stew is a wonderful comfort meal and a real crowd-pleaser. While cooking this stew, two of her cats tried to get up on the stove to take the lid off the pot! Please make sure that what happened to Ruthie doesn't happen in your house, no matter how good something smells or tastes. Keep your pets away from hot stoves! Leftovers of this stew can be frozen for up to 3 months or refrigerated for up to 4 days and rewarmed later.

1 pound chicken, cut into bite-sized pieces

3 cups chopped potatoes with skins on

1 cup chopped carrots

1 cup uncooked rice

1 cup chopped cauliflower

1 cup chopped broccoli

1 cup chopped green beans

¼ cup chopped fresh parsley, or 1⅓ tablespoons parsley flakes

¼ teaspoon kosher salt

1 cup uncooked egg noodles

1. Put the chicken, potatoes, carrots, and rice in a large stockpot. Add enough water to cover the ingredients completely and simmer for 45 minutes to 1 hour.

2. Add the cauliflower, broccoli, green beans, parsley, salt, and noodles and simmer for another ½ hour. When pierced with a fork, the meat juices should run clear. If not, continue to simmer until they do.

3. Let cool to room temperature and serve.

Barkin' Beef Stew

⅍ Makes 8 servings ⅍

I think of beef stew as the king of stews. I remember walking into my great-grandmother's New York City apartment as a little girl with its wonderful smell of something always cooking on the stove. Three dishes come to mind when I think of my great-grandmother: her beef stew, her chicken and apple soup, and her baked French toast, which was to die for. Here's my tribute to my great-grandmother: Barkin' Beef Stew. May your house always have a wonderful, cozy, home-cooked fragrance for you and your dogs to enjoy. I know that this recipe is a tail-wagging delight. It can be refrigerated for 4 days or frozen for 3 months in an airtight container.

4 tablespoons olive oil

2 pounds sirloin steak, cubed

2 cups cubed baby red potatoes

1 cup chopped carrots

4 cups beef broth

1 cup peas

1 cup chopped celery

½ cup corn

1 cup chopped green beans

¼ cup chopped zucchini

1 cup canned diced tomatoes

½ cup cooked baby elbow macaroni

1 tablespoon salt

3 tablespoons fresh parsley, or 1 tablespoon parsley flakes

1 tablespoon cornstarch mixed with 2 tablespoons warm water

1. In a large stockpot, heat the olive oil over medium-high heat. Add the steak and brown well on all sides.

2. Add the potatoes, carrots, and broth. Bring to a boil, cover, turn down the heat, and simmer until the potatoes are fork-tender, about 20 to 30 minutes.

3. Add the peas, celery, corn, green beans, zucchini, tomatoes, macaroni, salt, and parsley. Cover and simmer for 20 to 30 minutes.

4. Check to make sure that the meat is cooked through. When it is, turn up the heat to medium and slowly stir in the cornstarch mixture to thicken the stew.

5. Once the stew has thickened, remove from heat. Let cool and serve.

DR. KEVIN SAYS

Allergies in dogs are usually triggered by protein sources (beef, chicken, soy, and so on), and less often by carbohydrate sources (such as wheat or corn). If your dog is allergic to beef or chicken, try using a protein source that your dog has never eaten before. Salmon, venison, and duck are good examples of less popular proteins.

Red Snapper Stew

⸘ Makes 8 servings ⸘

Fish has the best ratio of omega-3 to omega-6 fatty acids, which helps reduce inflammation, minimizes allergies, and gives the coat a great luster. It's a great source of protein, and it's low in saturated fat. I tend to make this particular stew in small portions, as it will keep for only 1 to 2 days in the refrigerator or 1 month in the freezer.

2½ tablespoons olive oil

2 cups cubed skinned boneless red snapper (or salmon or trout)

2 cups peeled, parboiled, and cubed red potatoes

¾ cup fish stock

½ cup water

1 cup chopped green beans

½ cup peas

½ cup chopped carrots

¼ cup chopped fresh parsley, or 1⅓ tablespoons parsley flakes

¼ teaspoon kosher salt

1. In a large saucepan, heat the olive oil over medium heat.

2. Add the fish and cook for 3 to 6 minutes per side or until golden brown. Be sure to turn the fish over a few times during cooking to make sure that it browns evenly.

3. Add the potatoes, fish stock, water, vegetables, parsley, and salt. Cover and cook over low heat for 10 to 15 minutes or until all the vegetables are soft, but not mushy, when pierced with a fork. Let cool and then serve either warm or at room temperature.

Lovely Lamb Fricassee

〰 Makes 8 servings 〰

Carrots are a great source of vitamin A, an essential part of a dog's diet. Vitamin A is also found in dairy products, fish liver oil, liver, and other vegetables. Signs of vitamin A deficiency in dogs include poor-quality hair and skin, retarded growth, and night blindness. This dish freezes beautifully; it will keep for 5 days in the refrigerator or up to 3 months in the freezer.

4 tablespoons flour
1 pound lamb, cut into bite-sized pieces
2 tablespoons olive oil
1½ cups minced carrots
1½ cups peas
1½ cups corn
1½ cups peeled and chopped baby red potatoes
½ teaspoon salt
4 cups beef broth
3 tablespoons tomato paste

1. Put the flour in a bowl and dredge the lamb pieces in the flour. Shake off the excess and set the meat aside.

2. In a large stockpot, heat the oil over medium-low heat. Add the lamb and brown on all sides, about 5 to 10 minutes.

3. Add the carrots, peas, corn, potatoes, and salt and sauté for 5 minutes.

4. Add the beef broth, whisk in the tomato paste, and bring to a boil. Once it is boiling, turn the temperature way down, cover, and simmer for 1 hour.

5. Let cool and serve.

Nautical Navy Bean Soup

⚜ Makes 8 servings ⚜

In the late 1990s, I discovered that my dogs Governor and Senator loved beans. After I learned that beans are actually good for dogs, I decided to create a soup recipe for them. To this day, Little Man, Cappy, and Senny love my navy bean soup. This soup will keep in an airtight container for 5 days in the refrigerator or up to 3 months in the freezer. I never let my dogs eat the ham bone, but if I'm going to freeze the soup (or, for that matter, refrigerate it), I always store it with the ham bone in it because the bone continues to flavor the soup.

3½ quarts water, divided
2 whole tomatoes
1 pound (2 cups) dried navy beans
1 meaty ham bone, about 1½ pounds
1 cup cubed potatoes
1 cup thinly sliced celery
1 cup chopped carrots

1. In a saucepan, bring 1 quart water to a boil. Drop in one whole tomato, blanch for 3 minutes, and then drop the tomato into cold water. Repeat with the second tomato. Under cold water, peel the tomatoes. On a clean cutting board, cut the tomatoes in half and scoop out the seeds. Then dice the tomatoes and set them aside.

2. Bring 2½ quarts water to a boil in a large stockpot. Boil the beans for 2 minutes; then remove from heat and let them stand for 1 hour.

3. Add the ham bone to the beans, cover, and simmer for 2 hours or until almost tender.

4. Add the potatoes, celery, carrots, and blanched tomatoes and simmer for 1 hour longer.

5. Remove the ham bone, cut off the meat, dice it, and add the meat back to the beans. Let cool to room temperature and serve.

ALL ABOUT BLANCHING

Blanching is a cooking term that means to put a food into rapidly boiling water for 1 to 2 minutes, or until the skin starts to peel off, and then take it out and run it under cold water. Blanching is used to help remove the skin of tomatoes and some fruits. Placing them in very cold water right away stops the cooking process.

Cappy's Chicken and Apple Soup

⚜ Makes 8 servings ⚜

Earlier in this chapter, I talked about the three recipes my great-grandmother used to make. Many of my friends' mothers and grandmothers made chicken soup with fresh dill in it. I personally am not a big fan of the dill flavor. This may be because my great-grandmother's chicken soup had apples in it, which made for a salty-sweet flavor that I loved as a child. When my dog Cappy first came to me, I was told that he was 12 weeks old. After a few days, we went to the vet for his wellness checkup and first set of shots. To my and the vet's surprise, we found out that Cappy was only 5 or 6 weeks old. I took my little baby home with instructions on how to feed him, but I couldn't entice Cappy to eat, even from my hand. I quickly made a batch of this chicken and apple soup. He was still too young to eat the chicken or the apples, but I knew that by dipping my fingers into the broth, I could start down the road of bonding and stimulate his appetite. Today, Cappy is a healthy 7-year-old Yorkie. He weighs 4½ pounds but can outrun my Labrador and my Chihuahua. To this day, he will sit in the kitchen on a dog bed patiently waiting for chicken and apple soup. I hope you try this wonderful combination; it really is a heart-warmer. This soup will keep for 5 days in the refrigerator or up to 3 months in the freezer in an airtight container.

> 3-pound roasting chicken, quartered
>
> 2 quarts water
>
> 1½ cups chicken stock
>
> 2 teaspoons salt
>
> 2 cups chopped celery
>
> 2 cups chopped carrots
>
> 2 large apples, chopped
>
> 1 cup chopped green beans
>
> ¼ cup chopped fresh parsley, or 1⅓ tablespoons parsley flakes
>
> 4 cups uncooked egg noodles

1. Place the chicken and water in a large stockpot. Cover and simmer until tender, about 2½ hours.

2. Remove the chicken from the pot and strain the fat from the broth.

3. Let the chicken cool a bit, and then remove the skin and bones. Shred the meat into small pieces by pulling it apart with your hands. Use both white and dark meat. Then return the meat to the pot with the strained broth.

4. Add the chicken stock, salt, celery, carrots, apples, green beans, and parsley and cook until the vegetables are fork-tender, about 25 minutes.

5. Add the noodles and cook for 8 to 10 minutes or until the noodles are tender.

6. Let cool to room temperature and serve.

APPLE TIPS

Buy firm, well-colored apples and make sure that there are no mushy or brown spots on them. The skin should be tight. To keep chopped apples from turning brown, squeeze lemon or lime juice on the cut pieces.

Applesauce can be used as an all-natural sweetener in any of my soup, stew, or kibble recipes for dogs.

Hound Ham and Pea Soup

⁕ Makes 8 servings ⁕

I have ridden hunters and jumpers my whole life. Every Sunday in the fall, while riding in the ring and having my lesson, I would see the Bedford Hills Hunt Club—riders dressed to the nines, the horses beautifully groomed, and the dogs all running together. After the hunt, there was a huge brunch, and they served a great ham and pea soup. As a young teen, I would sneak into the club with my friends to join the meal. Here's my thank-you to the Bedford Hills Hunt Club: Hound Ham and Pea Soup. You can freeze this soup for 3 months or refrigerate it for 4 days.

> 1 ham bone or ham hock
> 2 quarts chicken stock or broth
> 1 cup split peas
> 8 Idaho potatoes, cubed
> 1 cup chopped cooked ham
> ½ cup chopped celery
> 1 cup fresh peas
> ¼ cup chopped fresh parsley, or 1⅓ tablespoons parsley flakes
> 1 cup uncooked egg noodles

1. In a large stockpot, combine the ham bone or hock with the chicken stock, split peas, and potatoes. Simmer for about 1 hour, skimming fat off the surface as necessary.

2. Take out half of the soup and purée it in a food processor or blender. Return it to pot and stir well so that everything is blended. This makes the soup thick and creamy.

3. Add the chopped ham, celery, fresh peas, parsley, and noodles. Return to a simmer for 10 to 15 minutes, or until the noodles are cooked through. Let cool, dispose of the cooked ham bone or hock (or store it with the soup in the refrigerator or freezer for flavor), and serve. Do *not* give your dog cooked bones.

Saucy Dog®

Saucy Dog is a registered trademark of mine, but I am giving you the original recipe here. You can turn Saucy Dog into a gravy or paint it on old toys to give them new life. You can also sprinkle it on your dog's food to add flavor. The great thing about Saucy Dog is that you can store it in a spice jar just like you do your spices. This recipe makes 2 large spice containers full and will keep for 1 month in the fridge or 6 months in the freezer. Finding the dried ingredients used to be difficult, but today they are more readily available at all-natural markets, at outdoor camping supply stores, and on the Internet. I usually buy 1 pound of each ingredient at a time and store it in the freezer.

1 cup freeze-dried liver
½ cup dried beef or chicken
½ cup low-salt or no-salt beef bouillon powder
½ cup parsley flakes
½ cup dried carrots
½ cup celery flakes
½ cup dried tomato flakes (if you can't find flakes, use dried diced tomatoes)
½ cup brewer's yeast (powdered or granular)
1 tablespoon red beet powder

1. Put the dried liver in a blender or food processor and blend into a powder. (I do this on the purée setting.) Set aside.

2. Put the dried beef or chicken into the blender or food processor and blend until the pieces are small enough to go through the holes in a spice jar lid, but are not puréed.

3. Add the dried liver powder and the bouillon powder to the beef or chicken pieces in the blender or food processor. Add the remaining ingredients and blend until you're happy with the consistency. I like to keep some small chunks.

3

Puglicious Pastas
and Loaves to Love

· ·

Pasta didn't really become popular in the U.S. until the late 1800s and early 1900s, when so many Italians immigrated to this country. Today, it is one of the most common dishes on the American dinner table. Pasta became popular in canned dog food in the late 1990s. It is a great source of healthy carbohydrates, a necessity for dogs. When I was in Italy in 1992, I was surprised to find a pet store in Florence offering 20-, 40-, and 60-pound bags of dried pasta—for dogs!

Loaves are among my favorite recipes to prepare for my boys. They are exceptionally easy to make, they freeze beautifully, and most of all, my dogs absolutely love them. The loaves in this chapter have fun twists to them that make them look really pretty when served and offer extra nutritional value. When I prepare these recipes, I like to use my silicone mini-loaf pan, which makes 12 mini-loaves, so that I end up with 12 convenient single servings. If you don't have a mini-loaf pan but want to make mini-loaves rather than one large loaf, spray your largest cookie sheet with nonstick cooking spray and fit as many freeform loaves in a row as you can. The average 9-x-12 cookie sheet will hold 6 loaves. You can also make one large freeform loaf in a 9-x-9 baking dish and slice it into single serving portions.

Turkey, Pasta, and Sweet Potato Dinner

〰️ Makes 8 servings 〰️

Try vegetable pasta when making this recipe—my dogs love spinach pasta. When the meatballs are done, I like to turn off the oven and let them sit in the oven awhile to dry out. Make sure not to burn them, but the longer you let them dry, the more intense the flavor becomes, and having less moisture in the food helps to preserve it. Store in an airtight container in the refrigerator for up to a week or in the freezer for up to 3 months.

2 cups cubed and boiled sweet potatoes

1¼ cups whole wheat flour

1 cup chicken broth

2 large eggs

2 turkey breasts, cooked and puréed

1 cup cooked pasta, any small shape

½ cup chopped fresh parsley, or 2⅔ tablespoons parsley flakes

½ cup canned crushed pineapple

4 tablespoons plain wheat germ

1 cup cooked millet (can be found at any health food store)

1 cup cooked and drained spinach (I use frozen chopped spinach and drain all the liquid by squeezing it in a paper towel)

1. Preheat the oven to 350 degrees. Spray a cookie sheet with nonstick cooking spray.

2. Mix together all the ingredients; the mixture should be a bit sticky.

3. Take a tablespoon of dough, roll it between your hands to make two balls, and place each ball on the cookie sheet.

4. Flatten the balls slightly with the back of a fork. Continue until all the mixture has been formed into balls.

5. Bake for 20 to 25 minutes or until golden brown. Remove from the oven, let cool, and serve.

DR. KEVIN SAYS

Sweet potatoes, like pumpkin, are a great source of insoluble fiber to help firm up the stool in dogs who frequently have loose stools.

Tomato-Lamb Orzo

⑅ Makes 8 servings ⑅

Orzo is small, rice-shaped pasta that can be found at any market. I love orzo because it's small, easy to cook, and easy to store, and you don't have the hassle of breaking the pasta into bite-sized pieces. I like to use whole wheat orzo for this recipe, if I can find it. You can refrigerate the leftovers of this dish for 3 to 4 days or freeze them in single-serving portions for up to 3 months.

    4 tablespoons olive oil
    2 pounds lamb, cubed
    ½ cup chopped zucchini
    ½ cup chopped green beans
    ½ cup peas
    1 cup canned chopped tomatoes
    4 tablespoons tomato sauce
    2 cups cooked orzo (follow package instructions)
    ¼ cup brewer's yeast

1. In a large saucepan, heat the olive oil over medium heat. Sauté the lamb in the oil until brown on the outside and cooked to medium (pale pink) on the inside, about 15 to 20 minutes.

2. Add the zucchini, green beans, and peas and sauté for 5 minutes.

3. Add the tomatoes and tomato sauce, turn down the heat, cover, and simmer for 10 minutes.

4. Check the meat to make sure that it is cooked through. Remove from heat, stir in the cooked orzo and brewer's yeast, and serve warm or at room temperature.

Daffy's Duck and Sweet Potato Loaf

If you can't find duck or you don't feel comfortable cooking with duck, this recipe works wonderfully with chicken or turkey. It will keep for 3 days in the refrigerator or up to 1 month in the freezer.

1 pound duck breast, cooked and shredded
2 cups cooked diced sweet potatoes
1 tablespoon olive oil
½ cup corn
¼ cup chopped fresh parsley, or 1⅓ tablespoons parsley flakes
½ cup plain dry bread crumbs
1 teaspoon salt
1 tablespoon brewer's yeast
½ teaspoon dark or light molasses
2 cups chicken stock
2 eggs, beaten

1. Preheat the oven to 350 degrees. Spray a loaf pan with nonstick cooking spray.

2. In a large mixing bowl, combine all the ingredients and blend well.

3. Place the mixture in the prepared loaf pan and bake for 45 minutes to 1 hour or until a knife inserted into the center comes out clean. Let cool, slice, and serve.

Little Man's Luscious Loaf

〰 Makes 12 servings 〰

This fun and easy recipe is one of my favorites—I make it at least once a month. These mini-loaves freeze beautifully for up to 3 months, and you can add everything but the kitchen sink. Not only does this recipe have a little extra protein boost, but when you slice open a mini-loaf, it's very pretty. From start to finish, it takes about 2 hours to prepare—well worth it for the joy you will see in your dog's face while he eats. I hope that your dog enjoys this recipe as much as my boys do.

3 raw eggs
2 pounds ground lamb
½ pound ground beef
2 cups cooked brown rice
¼ cup rolled oats
4 carrots, chopped
1 cup chopped green beans
½ cup chopped fresh parsley, or 2⅔ tablespoons parsley flakes
4 tablespoons plain wheat germ
2 tablespoons Worcestershire sauce
½ cup plain dry bread crumbs
12 hard-cooked eggs, shelled
2 tablespoons ketchup

1. Preheat the oven to 350 degrees. Spray a loaf pan with nonstick cooking spray.

2. In a mixing bowl, mix together everything except the hard-cooked eggs and ketchup.

3. Place a small amount of the meat mixture in the bottom of one section of the mini-loaf pan; then set a hard-cooked egg on top. Cover the egg with more of the meat mixture.

4. Repeat this process for the remaining mini-loaves. Not to worry—if your mini-loaf pan makes only 6, then make 6 small loaves at a time (meat, egg, meat). What you are doing is placing an egg in the center of the meat. When it's cooked and you slice it, it's beautiful.

   If you are making one large loaf instead of mini-loaves, make a well in the center of the loaf and add as many hard-cooked eggs as will fit into the well, in a line from one end of the loaf to the other.

5. Before placing in the oven, spread some ketchup on top of each mini-loaf.

6. Bake for 1 hour and 40 minutes or until a knife inserted into the center comes out clean. Remove from the oven, let cool for an hour, and serve.

STORING MINI-LOAVES

These loaves store fabulously in vacuum-sealed food storage bags. I love to use these because each loaf is sealed individually with all the moisture taken out, and they can be stored for 2 weeks in the refrigerator or 6 months in the freezer. If you don't have a vacuum-sealed food storage bag system, wrap each loaf very well in wax paper and aluminum foil, and then store in a zippered plastic bag for no more than a week in the refrigerator or 3 months in the freezer.

DR. KEVIN SAYS

A sudden intake of a very fatty meal can cause pancreatitis in dogs (as well as cats). Pancreatitis is a condition in which the pancreas is stimulated into overdrive, and the release of extra enzymes starts to digest the pancreas itself. We have kept regular bacon, organ meats, and other fatty foods out of the recipes in this book in order to make these meals low-fat and healthy.

Pork Roast and Apple Loaf

⚘ Makes 12 servings ⚘

This loaf freezes beautifully! It can be frozen for up to 3 months or refrigerated for 5 days in an airtight container. The recipe is fun and easy, and it takes only about 2 hours from start to finish.

3 eggs
2 pounds ground pork
½ pound ground beef
2 cups cooked brown rice
¼ cup rolled oats
¼ cup chopped fresh parsley, or 1⅓ tablespoons parsley flakes
4 carrots, chopped
1 cup chopped green beans
½ cup canned crushed pineapple
2 tablespoons Worcestershire sauce
½ cup plain dry bread crumbs
6 apples, peeled, seeds removed, and sliced into rounds
¼ cup freeze-dried apples
2 tablespoons ketchup

1. Preheat the oven to 350 degrees. Spray a loaf pan with nonstick cooking spray.

2. In a large mixing bowl, mix together everything except the apples and ketchup.

3. Place half of the meat mixture in the bottom of the loaf pan. Create a well in the center and pack it with the fresh apple slices. Place the rest of the meat mixture on top and blend the edges together to form one solid loaf.

4. Spread the ketchup on top and layer the dried apple slices over the ketchup. Push them into the loaf a bit so they don't fall off during cooking.

5. Bake for 2 hours or until a knife inserted into the center comes out clean. Remove from the oven, let cool for an hour, slice, and serve.

FREEZE-DRIED APPLE TIP

Freeze-dried apples give this recipe extra texture and fiber. Spray nonstick cooking spray on the blades of your knife, blender, or food processor before chopping dried fruit. Doing so will keep the fruit from sticking and makes cleanup a breeze.

DR. KEVIN SAYS

Carrots make great treats for a dog who just can't seem to keep the pounds off. They are low in calories and have a great crunch that most dogs enjoy. Be sure to use baby carrots, as large carrots may present a choking hazard.

Savory-Sweet Chicken and Apple Loaf

⚶ Makes 12 servings ⚶

We usually think of chicken as a savory dish, not a sweet dish. For example, a common recipe is roasted chicken with rosemary, lemon, and garlic. In this loaf, I have taken chicken and combined the two flavors of savory and sweet. The apple adds sweetness as well as natural fiber. The savory flavor comes from the cheese and brewer's yeast, which offer calcium and B vitamins. The carrots also add sweetness and are loaded with beta carotene. Because most dogs have a sweet tooth, this is a nice loaf to make for a finicky eater. This dish will keep for 5 days in the refrigerator or up to 3 months in the freezer. 4 cups finely chopped cooked chicken

    2 cups cooked rice
    1 cup soft bread crumbs
    ½ cup chopped fresh apples
    ¼ cup chopped fresh parsley, or 1⅓ tablespoons parsley flakes
    ½ cup canned crushed pineapple
    ½ teaspoon salt
    2 tablespoons brewer's yeast
    1½ cups chicken broth
    1 cup grated carrots
    ½ cup grated Monterey Jack cheese
    3 eggs, beaten
    ⅓ cup chopped dried apples

1. Preheat the oven to 350 degrees. Spray a loaf pan with nonstick cooking spray.

2. In a large mixing bowl, mix together everything except the dried apples and blend well.

3. Pack half of the chicken mixture firmly into the pan. Make a well in the center and pack it firmly with the dried apples, reserving 2 tablespoons for the top. Place the rest of the chicken mixture on top and blend the edges together to form one solid loaf. Sprinkle the remaining dried apples on top. Push them into the loaf a bit so they don't fall off during cooking.

4. Bake for 1 hour or until a knife inserted into the center comes out clean. Let cool, slice, and serve.

APPLE STORAGE TIP

Store fresh apples in a cool, dry, dark place and not near another fruit—sometimes that speeds up the ripening process.

ALL ABOUT PARSLEY

There are two types of parsley: flat-leaf and curly. Flat-leaf parsley, also called Italian parsley, is stronger in flavor. Curly parsley is milder in taste and is prettier. When picking parsley, look for bright green leaves and no browning.

When storing fresh parsley, wash it well, and then shake off the water and wrap the parsley in a dry paper towel. Placed in an airtight plastic bag, it will keep for up to a week in the refrigerator.

Thanksgiving for All Turkey Loaf

〜 Makes 12 servings 〜

I have many memories of getting up very early on Thanksgiving morning as a child in New York, my mother with her hands in the oven making one dish or another, and my father getting us kids ready to go to the Macy's Thanksgiving Day Parade. When I asked my mother why Thanksgiving was her favorite holiday, she answered that a) it was the time to give thanks to the people who founded this country, and b) it was a non-religious holiday that all Americans could celebrate. My mother was known for having a big feast—every year we had at least seventy people for a sit-down dinner. To this day, I always remember what a great childhood I had and what a great day Thanksgiving is. Our dogs always got to participate in Thanksgiving, and I have passed on the tradition to my boys. We celebrate every Thanksgiving together. This recipe is a great way to use up leftover turkey, and the boys can smell the turkey and sweet potatoes a mile away. You can refrigerate this loaf for up to 5 days, or freeze for up to 3 months.

6 cups cooked diced turkey

3 cups cooked, boiled, and cubed sweet potatoes

1 cup cooked brown rice

1 cup plain dry bread crumbs

1½ cups chopped green beans

1½ cups chopped carrots

1 cup canned crushed pineapple

2 eggs, beaten

1 tablespoon brewer's yeast

¼ cup chopped fresh parsley, or 1⅓ tablespoons parsley flakes

½ cup rolled oats

4 tablespoons plain wheat germ

1 tablespoon bone meal

½ teaspoon salt

5 tablespoons ketchup

1. Preheat the oven to 350 degrees. Spray a loaf pan with nonstick cooking spray.

2. In a large mixing bowl, combine all the ingredients except the ketchup.

3. Fill the prepared pan with the mixture and spread the ketchup over the top.

4. Bake for 1 hour or until a knife inserted into the center comes out clean. Let cool, slice, and serve.

ALL ABOUT BROWN RICE

Brown rice is the whole rice with the edible husk still on. It is a good source of fiber, vitamins, and texture. It has a nutty flavor, too.

4

Bulk Recipes and Budget Meals

· ·

THIS CHAPTER CONTAINS SOME REALLY FUN AND DIFFERENT RECIPES. I BET YOU WOULDN'T HAVE THOUGHT TO TRY FEEDING YOUR DOG FREEZE-DRIED FRUIT, YOGURT, AND COTTAGE CHEESE! MANY OF THESE RECIPES CAN BE MADE IN 1 DAY AND STORED IN THE FREEZER IN AIRTIGHT FREEZER BAGS FOR UP TO 3 MONTHS. ALL OF THESE RECIPES DOUBLE VERY WELL, TOO.

WHEN ON A BUDGET AND COOKING FOR YOUR PET, KEEP YOUR EYES OPEN FOR INGREDIENTS THAT ARE ON SALE AT YOUR ALL-NATURAL MARKET. I OFTEN BUY MEAT IN BULK, SEPARATE IT INTO PORTIONS IN VACUUM-SEALED STORAGE BAGS, AND FREEZE IT FOR LATER USE.

Wendy's Basic Bulk Recipe

⫶ Makes 12 servings ⫶

I make this big bulk recipe twice a month. My boys love it! To each serving, I add ¼ cup frozen blueberries for the antioxidants. The cottage cheese adds protein as well as natural calcium, which is easy for dogs to digest. This recipe will keep in the refrigerator for up to 5 days or in the freezer for up to 1 month.

3 tablespoons corn oil
1 pound ground turkey
4 chicken thighs, boiled, skin and bones removed, and shredded
28- or 30-ounce can organic tomatoes
28- or 30-ounce can no-salt-added green beans
14½- or 15-ounce can crushed pineapple
15-ounce jar unsweetened applesauce
1 cup rolled oats
1 cup cooked brown rice
28-ounce can pumpkin
½ cup plain wheat germ
1 cup chopped fresh parsley, or ⅓ cup parsley flakes
16-ounce container cottage cheese

1. In a large stockpot over medium to medium-high heat, heat the oil. Add the turkey and cook for 10 to 15 minutes. When the turkey is cooked through and starting to brown, add the chicken and cook until browned. Drain off the fat.

2. Add the tomatoes, green beans, pineapple, applesauce, oats, rice, pumpkin, wheat germ, and parsley. Bring to a boil, reduce the heat, and simmer for 5 minutes or until the oats are tender.

3. Let cool, stir in the cottage cheese, and serve.

Salmon and Rice

☙ Makes 8 servings ☙

Salmon is packed with omega-3 fatty acids, which can reduce triglycerides. This recipe can be made with fresh or canned salmon. I prefer to use canned; it lasts a long time. When you buy fresh fish, you need to cook it immediately. Refrigerate the leftovers of this disk for up to 3 days, or freeze for up to 1 month.

        2 tablespoons olive oil
        1 cup canned chopped tomatoes
        ½ cup chopped zucchini
        ½ cup chopped green beans
        ½ cup peas
        2 9-ounce cans salmon in oil
        1½ cups cooked brown rice
        3 tablespoons plain wheat germ
        ¼ cup chopped fresh parsley, or 1⅓ tablespoons parsley flakes
        ½ cup fish stock

1. In a saucepan over medium-high heat, heat the olive oil. Add the tomatoes, zucchini, green beans, and peas and sauté until fork-tender, about 15 to 20 minutes.

2. Add the salmon, rice, wheat germ, parsley, and fish stock. Stir well and sauté for 5 more minutes. Let cool and serve.

DR. KEVIN SAYS

Salmon and trout must be cooked well to avoid salmon poisoning, a parasitic condition transmitted from snails, which can make dogs very sick. Never serve freshly caught Pacific Coast fish to your pet without cooking it thoroughly. Dogs should not eat raw fish.

Wendy's Cheesy Meatballs

⸱ Makes 8 servings ⸱

You can make your meatballs any size you want, and they can be ready in a pinch. They freeze beautifully and will last up to 3 months in the freezer or 5 days in the refrigerator.

2 pounds ground beef
2 cups shredded Cheddar cheese
1 cup chopped green beans
1 cup chopped carrots
1 cup peas
½ cup rolled oats
½ cup chopped fresh parsley, or 2⅔ tablespoons parsley flakes
½ teaspoon kosher salt
2 cups cooked brown rice
1½ cups Parmesan cheese
8 tablespoons plain wheat germ
8 teaspoons olive oil

1. Preheat the oven to 350 degrees.

2. In a large mixing bowl, mix together the ground beef, Cheddar cheese, vegetables, rolled oats, parsley, salt, and rice.

3. In another mixing bowl, mix together the Parmesan cheese and wheat germ.

4. Take a heaping tablespoon of the meat mixture and roll it into a meatball shape; then roll it in the Parmesan–wheat germ mixture. Repeat with the remaining meat mixture. You should end up with 20 to 40 medium-sized meatballs.

5. Heat the olive oil in a sauté pan over medium-high heat. Sauté the meatballs in the oil for about 15 minutes, or until a nice golden crust forms to seal in the juices. The meatballs will continue browning and will cook through in the oven.

6. Place the meatballs in a Pyrex baking dish and bake for 1 hour. Let cool and serve.

ALL ABOUT BEEF

The United States Department of Agriculture (USDA) grades beef on three factors: 1) confirmation (the portion of meat to bone); 2) finish (the portion of fat to lean meat), and 3) overall quality. The UDSA's three top grades are prime, choice, and select. These grades are what are commonly available to us as consumers. Prime beef is usually found in upscale meat shops and supermarkets and at fine restaurants.

When it comes to buying beef, choose meats that are bright red in color. Make sure that the cut you purchase has marbling—flecks or streaks of fat in the meat, which make it tender—but not too much. When storing beef, keep it in airtight packaging. If you are wrapping ground beef to freeze it, leave it in the shrink-wrap, and then wrap it for the freezer. Meat should be kept in the coldest part of the refrigerator, and only for 2 days. When wrapped in airtight packaging, beef will keep for up to 3 months in the freezer.

If you can't find all-natural beef—made without growth hormones, antibiotics, and other chemicals—opt for prime or choice cuts.

Chicken and Rice with Apples

⚬ Makes 8 servings ⚬

The apples give this recipe a kick of natural sweetness as well as fiber. You can make the rice ahead of time—it will keep in the fridge for 5 days, as will the finished recipe. This dish should be served at room temperature or warm, but never hot. You can freeze the leftovers for up to 3 months in an airtight container.

1 tablespoon olive oil

¼ teaspoon kosher salt

2 cups chopped carrots

½ cup chopped tomatoes (fresh or canned all-natural)

1 cup chopped green beans

2 apples, cored and chopped

1 cup corn (fresh or canned)

8 cups cooked chicken cut into strips, cubed, or shredded (I boil my chicken for this recipe)

6 cups cooked brown rice

½ cup rolled oats

4 tablespoons plain wheat germ

¼ cup chopped fresh parsley, or 1⅓ tablespoons parsley flakes

¼ cup dried apples

1. In a large sauté pan, heat the olive oil over medium-high heat. Add the salt, carrots, tomatoes, green beans, chopped apples, and corn, and sauté in the oil for 5 minutes.

2. Reduce the heat and simmer for another 2 to 3 minutes; then remove from heat and let cool. You should have liquid in the pan from the tomatoes. If there is no liquid in the pan, add a couple of tablespoons of chicken broth or water.

3. In a large mixing bowl, combine the chicken, rice, oats, wheat germ, parsley, and dried apples with the sautéed vegetables and fruit. Serve.

Tuna Tostadas

Makes 6 servings

I live in southern California, an area famous for its south-of-the-border cuisine. Mexican food is my favorite—I could eat it 7 days a week. Lucky for me, Mexican cuisine is found everywhere in California. If you're not familiar with Mexican food, be daring and give this recipe a try. You and your pets can try it together! This is a great recipe for both dogs and cats. It can be refrigerated for 2 days; do not freeze it.

6 corn tortillas
2 cans dark tuna in oil
½ cup chopped tomatoes
½ cup corn
2 tablespoons chopped red bell pepper
2 tablespoons tomato paste
½ cup grated Cheddar cheese
fresh parsley for garnish (optional)

1. Preheat the oven to 400 degrees. Spray a cookie sheet with nonstick cooking spray.

2. Place the tortillas on the cookie sheet and bake or broil until brown and crispy, about 3 to 4 minutes for baking or 1 minute for broiling. Watch them closely so they don't burn. Turn them over about halfway through baking so they brown on both sides.

3. Add the tuna, tomatoes, corn, and bell pepper to a sauté pan and sauté over medium heat for 5 minutes. Add the tomato paste and cook for an additional 5 minutes to help thicken the mixture.

4. Break up one tortilla over each serving to add crunch; then sprinkle with a little bit of the cheese. Garnish with parsley if you like, and it's ready to serve!

Chicken and Ham Pockets

I like to use leftover meat for this recipe. You can substitute turkey or lamb for the chicken, and you can make whatever size pockets you want. The pockets freeze great—they will keep for 5 days in the fridge or 3 months in an airtight container in the freezer.

FILLING

3 cups diced cooked chicken

3 cups diced cooked ham

3 cups cubed, boiled, and mashed sweet potatoes

¼ cup chopped fresh parsley, or 1⅓ tablespoons parsley flakes

1 cup cooked brown rice

1½ cups chopped green beans

1½ cups chopped carrots

1 tablespoon brewer's yeast

1 tablespoon bone meal

½ teaspoon salt

3 tablespoons butter

2 eggs, beaten

In a large mixing bowl, mix together all the filling ingredients. Set aside.

CRUST

⅔ cup shortening

2 cups flour

2 teaspoons baking powder

½ teaspoon salt

3 to 5 tablespoons very cold water

10 cups chicken broth or water, or a combination

1. Cut the shortening into the flour. Add the baking powder and salt and mix until it looks like coarse cornmeal.

2. Add 3 to 5 tablespoons cold water, enough to make your dough the right consistency for rolling—you don't want it to be too sticky. Pinch out a piece of dough and flatten it with your hands. If it flattens easily, it is ready for rolling.

3. On a lightly floured surface, roll the dough to ¼-inch thickness and then cut it into 4- to 5-inch squares. You don't have to be perfect here.

4. Put 2 tablespoons of the filling inside each square. Fold the dough over and use the back of a fork or your fingers to pinch it closed.

5. Set a large stockpot filled with the chicken broth or water on the stove to boil. When all your pockets are formed, drop the pockets into the boiling broth.

6. Cover, reduce heat, and simmer for 25 minutes. Remove the pockets from the broth and let cool. To serve, take the appropriate number of pockets for your dog and pour some broth over the top. For example, I give my little dogs, Cappy and Little Man, two cut-up pockets with ½ cup broth, and I give my Labrador, Senny, four to five cut-up pockets with 1 cup broth. Store the pockets and the broth separately.

Yogurt and Fruit

Makes 4 servings

You'll be surprised to see how much your dog will love fruit and yogurt. This is a nice sweet treat that contains protein, fiber, and antioxidants. I never freeze this dish; it will keep for 1 to 2 days in the refrigerator. It must be kept covered, or the bananas and apples will turn brown.

2 cups cooked rolled oats

1 cup lowfat cottage cheese

1 cup plain nonfat yogurt

3 tablespoons plain wheat germ

1 teaspoon flaxseed

½ cup blueberries

½ cup diced apple

½ cup chopped banana

¼ cup dried apples

2 tablespoons olive oil

Combine all the ingredients in a large mixing bowl and serve!

Variation: Add 1 hard-cooked egg, peeled and chopped, for extra protein.

All About Blueberries

Blueberries are low in calories, low in fat, packed with vitamins and minerals, and contain bioflavonoids, which help reduce the likelihood of hemorrhaging. When selecting blueberries, make sure that they are plump, firm, uniform in size, and have a frosted blue color. Refrigerate your blueberries tightly covered. They will last in the coldest part of the fridge for up to 10 days, or in the freezer in an airtight container for up to 2 months. Remove the stems and wash the blueberries on the day you actually use them.

Part II: *Cats*

5

Kibbles and Casseroles

Cats are even more prone to tartar buildup and gingivitis than dogs are. Because kibble helps minimize the formation of plaque and tartar, it is an important part of a cat's diet. Making homemade kibble is as simple as making treats for your cat. The basic dough recipe is similar; it's the extra ingredients you add that give each kibble a unique twist. For example, apples go well with turkey or chicken. Fish flakes and broccoli go well with fish. Adding fish flakes or 1 tablespoon of Thai fish sauce to a fish-based kibble will intensify the fish flavor.

The hardest part about making your own kibble is finding the time to let it dry out in the oven. Letting it sit in an off oven overnight is best. This important step helps concentrate the kibble's flavor and makes it keep longer. If moisture gets to it, it can become moldy and soft. This is why I make small batches at a time.

Homemade kibble can be stored in an airtight container in the refrigerator for a week or in the freezer for up to 3 months. I seal 6 cups in a vacuum-sealed food storage bag and freeze it. When I need it, I take out a bag and store it in the refrigerator. The great thing about vacuum-sealed food storage systems is that you can reseal opened bags, removing air again, which keeps food fresher longer.

Casseroles are nice complements to kibbles. You can mix together a bit of each, just as you would mix commercial kibble and canned cat food. The recipes in this chapter use an assortment of protein sources, but for variety, or if your cat has allergies, you can substitute other proteins, such as fish, beef, chicken, turkey, or lamb.

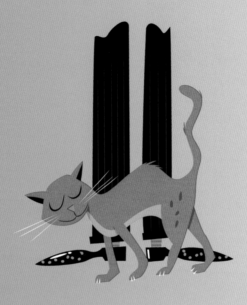

Champion Cat Turkey Kibble

⚶ Makes 10 to 20 servings ⚶

Here's a classic kibble that any cat will love. I like to use 18-x-13-inch cookie sheets, usually available at cooking supply stores, so that I can fit more into the oven at one time. You may need to make your kibble in batches, especially if you use smaller cookie sheets. If so, transfer the first batch to a shallow baking pan, let your cookie sheets cool, and then bake the second batch. When all the kibble has been baked, put it all back into the oven, now turned off, to let it dry out. You can freeze it for up to 3 months or refrigerate it for up to a week in an airtight container.

3 cups whole wheat flour
2 cups rye flour
1 cup plain wheat germ
1 cup cornmeal
1 cup nonfat dry milk
3 tablespoons parsley flakes
½ cup brewer's yeast
2 pounds cooked turkey
1 cup water
5 tablespoons vegetable oil
1 tablespoon cod liver oil
1 cup dried fish flakes

1. Preheat the oven to 350 degrees. Spray two large cookie sheets with nonstick cooking spray.

2. In a large mixing bowl, combine the flours, wheat germ, cornmeal, dry milk, parsley, flakesand brewer's yeast.

3. In a blender or food processor, blend the turkey, water, and oils until smooth.

4. Add the turkey mixture to the dry ingredients and mix thoroughly. If the dough is too tough, add water as needed to make the dough firm and smooth.

5. Use your hands and a big flat spatula to flatten the dough out on the cookie sheets to a thickness of ¼ to ½ inch. If you want to roll out the dough, feel free to do so, but I find it easier to use my hands. Then score it into small pieces with a knife. You can make your kibble any shape you want—be creative!

6. Sprinkle with fish flakes and bake for 25 to 35 minutes or until the kibble is golden brown and not doughy when you break a piece open. During the baking process, take a wooden spoon or spatula and move the kibble around on the cookie sheet so that it bakes evenly.

7. Turn off the oven, keeping the door closed. Let the kibble dry out in the off oven for at least 4 to 6 hours or overnight. The longer you allow your kibble to sit in the oven, the drier and more flavorful it will become, and the longer it can be stored.

8. Remove the kibble from the oven. It will still be slightly warm and moist. Let it sit on cooling racks for another hour or two until it is completely dry and cool.

Variation: Substitute fish, beef, chicken, or lamb for the turkey. Simply boil the meat until cooked through, drain it well, purée it, and then add it to your kibble.

ALL ABOUT FISH FLAKES

The Japanese word for prepared, dried, and smoked tuna fish flakes is *katsuobushi*. It is often one of the main ingredients in soups, sauces, and stews. It is typically found in bags of small pink-brown shavings that look somewhat like cedar shavings. Fish flakes are also used as a flavoring and topping for many Japanese dishes. When added as a topping to a hot dish, the flakes appear to be dancing. In Japan, they call them dancing fish flakes. You can purchase fish flakes at an Asian market, a specialty cooking store, online, and at many large supermarkets. Look in the foreign foods aisle.

Kitty Fish Kibble

Makes 10 to 20 servings

This is an excellent recipe if you have a finicky cat. It uses canned mackerel, which is high in omega-3 fatty acids. It also has an intense smell and flavor, which will entice your cat to eat. If you can't find mackerel, feel free to substitute another canned fish—try salmon, sardines, or whitefish for variety. Store in an airtight container in the refrigerator for up to a week, or freeze for up to 3 months.

3 cups whole wheat flour

2 cups rye flour

1 cup plain wheat germ

1 cup cornmeal

1 cup nonfat dry milk

3 tablespoons parsley flakes

½ cup brewer's yeast

½ cup dried fish jerky, chopped in a blender (but not puréed)

2 cups dried fish flakes, divided

15-ounce can mackerel

5 tablespoons vegetable oil

1 tablespoon cod liver oil

2 tablespoons Thai fish sauce

1 cup water, or as needed

1. Preheat the oven to 350 degrees. Spray two large cookie sheets with nonstick cooking spray.

2. In a large mixing bowl, mix together the flours, wheat germ, cornmeal, dry milk, parsley flakes, brewer's yeast, chopped fish jerky, and 1 cup of the fish flakes.

3. In another bowl, mash the mackerel into small pieces. Mix in the oils, Thai fish sauce, and 1 cup water. Put the mixture in a blender or food processor and purée well.

4. Add the puréed mackerel mixture to the dry ingredients and mix thoroughly. If the dough is too tough, add water as needed to make the dough firm and smooth.

5. Use your hands and a big flat spatula to flatten out the dough on the cookie sheets to a thickness of ¼ to ½ inch. Then score it into small pieces with a knife.

6. Sprinkle with the remaining 1 cup dried fish flakes and bake for 25 minutes or until the kibble is golden brown and not doughy when you break a piece open. During the baking process, take a wooden spoon or spatula and move the kibble around on the cookie sheet so that it bakes evenly.

7. Turn off the oven, keeping the door closed. Let the kibble dry out in the off oven for at least 4 to 6 hours or overnight. The longer you allow your kibble to sit in the oven, the drier and more flavorful it will become, and the longer it can be stored.

8. Remove the kibble from the oven. It will still be slightly warm and moist. Let it sit on cooling racks for another hour or two until it is completely dry and cool.

A Great Gift!

At holiday time, I make several batches of kibble to give as gifts. I take 6 to 10 cups of kibble and seal it in a vacuum-sealed food storage bag. Then I make a homemade label with the cat's name, the name of the recipe, and the date I made the kibble, along with instructions for using and storing it. I put it in a small basket lined with tissue paper along with a small homemade scratching post, which I make by taking a dowel rod that is 4 to 6 inches in diameter and 10 inches long and rolling sisal around it. I secure the sisal with either nontoxic glue or staples and, after the glue has dried, glue the post to a base made from a 2-x-2-foot piece of plywood. Once that dries, I set the post bottom side up in the basket with the kibble and wrap with a large bow and gift tag.

Cheese and Eggs Casserole

⋙ Makes 4 servings ⋘

Cheese and eggs are great sources of protein, and yogurt is a wonderful source of calcium that assists in bone building. You'll be surprised to see how easy this nutrient-rich recipe is to make. I do not freeze this casserole; I always make it fresh. It will keep in the refrigerator for 1 to 2 days.

4 eggs, beaten
½ cup grated Monterey Jack cheese
4 tablespoons plain yogurt
1 tablespoon plain wheat germ
1 teaspoon brewer's yeast
½ teaspoon salt
1 tablespoon corn oil

1. In a medium mixing bowl, blend all the ingredients except the corn oil.

2. In a large skillet over medium heat, heat the corn oil. Add the egg and cheese mixture, reduce the heat, and scramble until the eggs are cooked through. Let cool and serve.

FREEZER TIP

Be sure to remove all the air from your container before storing food in the freezer; doing so helps keep the food fresh and prevents freezer burn.

Fabulous Fish Casserole

〰 Makes 6 servings 〰

This recipe features oat or wheat grass. These grasses are safe for cats and help with the passage of hairballs and with digestion, adding extra fiber in a safe manner. Neither type of grass is harsh on a cat's stomach as the grass from your yard is. Feeding a cat grass can protect houseplants that the cat might be tempted to eat, as some plants look like grass to a cat—asparagus ferns, spider plants, and dracenea, to name a few. I call for a casserole dish, but you can use a loaf pan if you prefer. This casserole can be stored in the refrigerator for 1 to 2 days or frozen for up to 1 month. You can also freeze the prepared casserole for 3 months or refrigerate 4 for 3 days.

½ pound tuna or sole, cubed and deboned
½ pound sardines packed in tomato sauce
½ cup cooked brown rice
½ cup oat grass or wheat grass
¼ cup chopped fresh parsley, or 1⅓ tablespoons parsley flakes
2 eggs, beaten
2 tablespoons milk
4 tablespoons Parmesan cheese

1. Preheat the oven to 350 degrees. Spray a casserole dish with nonstick cooking spray.

2. In a large mixing bowl, combine the fish, rice, grass, and parsley.

3. In a separate bowl, mix together the eggs and milk.

4. Place the fish mixture in the prepared casserole dish, and then pour the egg mixture over it. Sprinkle the Parmesan cheese on top.

5. Bake for 30 minutes or until a knife inserted into the center comes out clean. Let cool and serve.

Gobble, Gobble Turkey Casserole

⚘ Makes 6 servings ⚘

This recipe is especially great around holiday time. I often have leftover turkey that I never know what to do with. A great tip is to chop your leftover turkey and freeze it in 8-ounce bags. That way, when you're ready to make a dish, you can pull an exact portion out of the freezer. You can also freeze the prepared casserole for 3 months or refrigerate it for 3 days.

1 pound cooked turkey, cut into bite-sized pieces or shredded
8-ounce can corn, drained
8-ounce can sliced carrots, drained, or 1 pound fresh carrots, cooked
8-ounce can clam chowder
1 cup cooked brown rice
1 tablespoon plain wheat germ
¼ cup chopped fresh parsley, or 1⅓ tablespoons parsley flakes
½ teaspoon brewer's yeast

1. Preheat the oven to 350 degrees. Spray a large casserole dish with nonstick cooking spray.

2. Stir all the ingredients together and place in the casserole dish.

3. Cover and cook for 25 minutes or until heated through; a knife inserted into the center should come out clean. Let cool and serve.

RICE PREPARATION HINTS

Rice is very good for pets, so I use a lot of rice in my recipes. Investing in a rice cooker makes life easier; all you need is a basic model. If you must cook your rice on the stove, never lift the cover of the pot once the cooking process has started—doing so will ruin the rice. I have lost many pots of rice by lifting the cover too soon. Follow the box instructions closely!

Salmon Casserole

Makes 4 to 6 servings

Salmon is a great source of protein and omega-3 fatty acids. I also add wheat germ and brewer's yeast to this recipe, both of which contain a lot of complex B vitamins. The nice thing about this casserole is that it freezes beautifully. It will keep for 2 days in the refrigerator or up to 1 month in the freezer.

16-ounce can salmon, drained
3 cups plain dry bread crumbs
¼ cup chopped carrots
¼ cup chopped fresh parsley, or 1⅓ tablespoons parsley flakes
2 tablespoons brewer's yeast
2 tablespoons plain wheat germ
3 eggs, beaten
½ cup milk
¼ cup corn oil
2 tablespoons fish flakes

1. Preheat the oven to 350 degrees. Spray a loaf pan with nonstick cooking spray.

2. In a large mixing bowl, add the drained salmon, bread crumbs, carrots, parsley, brewer's yeast, and wheat germ and mix very well.

3. Add the eggs, milk, and corn oil and blend well.

4. Spread the mixture in the loaf pan and sprinkle the fish flakes on top.

5. Bake for 45 minutes to 1 hour or until a knife inserted into the center comes out clean. Let cool and serve.

Variation: Anchovy paste can be used to flavor any fish dish, stew, or soup. A little bit goes a long way.

6

Stupendous Stews, Savory Soups, and Scrumptious Sauces

· ·

BEFORE THE PET FOOD RECALL, I WAS A BIG ADVOCATE OF WELL-MADE DRY CAT FOOD, KNOWN AS KIBBLE. KIBBLE HELPS KEEP YOUR PET'S TEETH CLEAN, OFFERS THE VITAMINS AND MINERALS NEEDED IN A DAILY DIET, AND IS FAIRLY INEXPENSIVE AS THE BULK PORTION OF A MEAL. I STILL FEED COMMERCIAL KIBBLE TO MY PETS, ALTHOUGH I CHOOSE CAREFULLY. I HAVE NEVER BEEN A PROPONENT OF THE CANNED PET FOODS AND PREMADE GRAVIES ON THE MARKET, HOWEVER. THIS IS WHERE HOMEMADE SOUPS, STEWS, AND GRAVIES COME INTO PLAY. IF YOUR CAT LOVES WET FOOD, YOU WILL FIND SOME WONDERFUL AND EASY RECIPES IN THIS CHAPTER TO REPLACE THE MOIST CANNED FOOD YOU MAY BE FEEDING NOW.

ALTHOUGH THE DIRECTIONS I GIVE ARE FOR COOKING ON THE STOVETOP, ALL THE RECIPES IN THIS CHAPTER CAN BE PREPARED IN A SLOW COOKER. FOR SLOW COOKER INSTRUCTIONS, SEE PAGE 18 IN CHAPTER 2. ALMOST EVERY RECIPE IN THIS CHAPTER, WITH ONLY A FEW EXCEPTIONS, FREEZES BEAUTIFULLY IN SINGLE-SERVING PORTIONS AND WILL LAST ANYWHERE FROM 1 TO 3 MONTHS IN THE FREEZER. THE RECIPES YOU CAN'T FREEZE WILL KEEP FOR AT LEAST A FEW DAYS IN THE REFRIGERATOR SO THAT YOU CAN COOK ONCE AND FEED YOUR CAT SEVERAL SPECIAL MEALS. BON APPÉTIT!

Funky Fish Stew

⫻ Makes 8 servings ⫻

Cats love fish. It's a great source of protein and omega-3 fatty acids, which are great for their coats. If you can't find fish stock, use bottled clam juice. I tend to make small portions of this stew; it will keep for only 1 to 2 days in the refrigerator or 1 month in the freezer.

> 2 tablespoons olive oil
> 2 10-ounce cans salmon, drained, liquid reserved
> 1 cup baby red potatoes, parboiled
> ½ cup chopped green beans
> ½ cup peas
> 1 cup cooked brown rice
> ¼ cup chopped fresh parsley, or 1⅓ tablespoons parsley flakes
> 2 cups fish stock
> ½ cup water

1. In a large stockpot, heat the olive oil over medium heat. Sauté the salmon in the oil for 3 to 5 minutes or until just heated through.

2. Add the remaining ingredients and bring to a boil. Cover and simmer for 10 minutes, or until the potatoes are fork-tender. Serve warm or at room temperature.

ALL ABOUT PARBOILING

Parboiling is a method of cooking foods partway through. It is used for foods that are dense in texture, like carrots and potatoes. Place your veggies in rapidly boiling water to partially cook; then plunge them in ice-cold water to stop the cooking process.

Ravenous Rabbit Stew

⸙ Makes 8 servings ⸙

When buying meat for this stew, know the difference between rabbits and hares. Rabbits are plumper and usually have a less gamey flavor. Hares have a stronger flavor, and the meat usually has to be tenderized before cooking, while rabbit does not. Try to get a younger rabbit weighing between 2 and 2½ pounds. The flesh will be lightly colored and more tender, with a milder flavor. This dish will keep for 5 days in the refrigerator or 3 months in the freezer.

  2 tablespoons safflower oil
  1 pound rabbit (or other meat), cubed
  6 small carrots, sliced very thin
  ½ cup peeled cubed sweet potatoes
  ¼ cup lentils
  ½ teaspoon salt
  8 cups beef broth
  1 teaspoon brewer's yeast
  1 tablespoon cornstarch mixed with 1 tablespoon warm water
  ½ cup chopped fresh parsley

1. In a large stockpot or slow cooker, heat the oil over medium-high heat. Add the meat and brown it in the oil.

2. Add the carrots, sweet potatoes, lentils, salt, beef broth, and brewer's yeast. Bring to a boil, cover, and simmer for 45 minutes.

3. Add the cornstarch-water mixture, bring to a boil, and cook for 2 minutes, whisking constantly. This will help thicken your sauce.

4. Remove from heat and add the parsley. Let cool and serve.

Variation: Substitute beef, chicken, turkey, or lamb for the rabbit.

Prowling Goulash

Makes 8 servings

Goulash, the national dish of Hungary, is also known as shepherd stew. A goulash recipe always contains paprika. This version is very easy to prepare; you can make it in a stockpot or a slow cooker. This dish will keep for 5 days in the refrigerator or up to 3 months in the freezer.

2 teaspoons olive oil
1 pound lean ground beef
16-ounce can tomatoes
½ cup water
¼ cup chopped spinach
¼ cup chopped celery
1½ teaspoons salt
½ teaspoon paprika
1 teaspoon brewer's yeast
1½ cups uncooked fine noodles (about 3 ounces)
1 tablespoon flour

1. In a large stockpot over medium-high heat, heat the olive oil. Add the beef and brown well. Drain the beef and return it to the pot.

2. Add the tomatoes, water, spinach, celery, salt, paprika, and brewer's yeast and bring to a boil. Reduce the heat, cover, and simmer for 1 hour over very low heat.

3. Add the noodles and cook until the noodles are done, about 15 minutes.

4. Add the flour and whisk for 3 minutes to thicken the sauce, making sure to blend the flour well. Let cool and serve.

STEW AND SOUP STORAGE

Here's a great tip that I read once. Save old milk or juice cartons (the 8-ounce size is best). Wash and dry them very well. Cut a carton to the size you need and pour your soup or stew inside. Then put the filled carton in a zippered freezer bag and store it in the freezer. If you stand it up in the freezer until frozen, it won't spill when you place it in the bag for storage. You can empty the carton contents into a saucepan to defrost. Do not put the carton in the microwave.

DR. KEVIN SAYS

Cats rely heavily on their sense of smell when tasting any new food. If your cat seems hesitant to try a new food, try putting it right in front of her nose for a few seconds and see if that entices her to try it. For a cat, "smelly" food is not always a bad thing.

Cape Cod Chowder

While I was in college, I spent almost every summer on Cape Cod. I always anticipated that wonderful warm bowl of New England clam chowder. Even on a hot summer evening, this soup was just delicious. As I began thinking up recipes for cats, I realized that our feline friends would love this dish, too! As a general rule, clam chowder does not freeze well because the potatoes become mushy and the soup part of the chowder separates. Professionally frozen clam chowder uses something called flash freezing, which freezes faster than your home freezer can. I suggest that you store any leftovers in the refrigerator in an airtight container for no more than 7 days.

2 10½-ounce cans minced clams (or 3 6½-ounce cans)
⅛ teaspoon corn oil
2½ cups peeled and chopped potatoes
1 cup chopped corn
3 cups water
3 cups clam juice or fish broth
1 pound frozen haddock fillets
1 teaspoon Worcestershire sauce
1½ cups milk
3 tablespoons cornstarch
1½ cups light cream
¼ cup chopped fresh parsley, or 1⅓ tablespoons parsley flakes
2 teaspoons dried fish flakes

1. Drain the clams, reserving the juice.

2. Heat the oil in a stockpot over medium-high heat. Sauté the potatoes in the oil for 10 minutes; then add the corn and sauté for another 10 minutes.

3. Add the water and clam juice or fish stock. If you don't have 3 cups of clam juice from the canned clams, supplement with bottled clam juice or canned fish broth. Bring to a boil, reduce the heat, and simmer for 10 minutes.

4. Add the haddock fillets, clams, and Worcestershire sauce. Bring to a boil, reduce the heat, cover, and simmer for 8 minutes or until the potatoes are fork-tender.

5. Remove the haddock and cut it into small pieces.

6. Slightly smash the potatoes with a fork.

7. In a small bowl, stir together the milk and cornstarch. Add the cream and then add to the potato mixture. Cook, stirring frequently, until thickened and bubbly.

8. Stir in the haddock. Return to a boil, reduce the heat, and cook for about 10 minutes, whisking frequently to prevent sticking.

9. Let cool, garnish with the parsley and fish flakes, and serve.

DR. KEVIN SAYS

It is a misconception that adult cats—or even kittens, for that matter—require a bowl of milk every day. In fact, many cats are somewhat intolerant of dairy and can easily get diarrhea from an overabundance of dairy products.

Sassy Sardine Soup

Makes 4 to 6 servings

My stepmother is Norwegian, so I spent some time in Norway growing up. Norwegians eat a lot of salmon and sardines, which pack a lot of omega-3 fatty acids and calcium. I remember saying no to sardines as a little girl, until I tried them with cream cheese on a bagel. From that day forward I was a sardine fan. This dish will keep for 3 days in the refrigerator or 1 month in the freezer.

2 15-ounce cans sardines
1 tablespoon butter
1 cup fish stock, vegetable stock, or water
¼ cup cooked brown rice
1 teaspoon brewer's yeast
6 stalks watercress
fresh parsley for garnish

1. Put the sardines and butter in a heavy-based frying pan and cook over medium heat, stirring continuously. As the pan warms and the butter melts, mash the sardines into it.

2. When the butter has melted completely, pour in the fish stock and stir as it comes to a boil.

3. Reduce the heat to a simmer. Add the rice and brewer's yeast and simmer for 5 minutes.

4. Thoroughly chop the watercress and toss it into the pan. Remove the pan from heat and let cool.

5. Purée the cooled mixture in a blender or food processor, add some parsley for garnish, and serve.

Grandma's Chicken Soup

Chicken soup is a great dish to serve when your kitty is not feeling her best. This nice bland recipe will hydrate your cat and offer her a good source of protein. It can be refrigerated for 7 days or frozen for up to 3 months. When you reheat it, bring it to a boil and then turn down the heat and simmer for 5 to 8 minutes. I like to freeze this soup in 8-ounce containers so that I can pull out 1 serving at a time.

2 quarts chicken stock or broth
1 whole chicken
¼ cup coarsely chopped green beans
½ cup coarsely chopped carrots
½ cup finely chopped celery
¾ cup corn
¼ cup chopped fresh parsley, or 1⅓ tablespoons parsley flakes
1 cup uncooked egg noodles

1. In a large stockpot, combine the chicken stock, chicken, green beans, carrots, and celery.

2. Bring to a simmer and simmer for about 1 hour, skimming fat off the surface as necessary.

3. Let cool. When the chicken is cool enough to handle, cut it into neat little pieces or shred it and return it to the pot. Add the corn and parsley to the broth.

4. Return the soup to a simmer for 15 to 30 minutes. Add the noodles during last 15 minutes of cooking. Remove from heat and let cool; then serve or freeze.

Fish-Flavored Sauce

⚡ Makes 1 cup, or about 3 servings ⚡

I serve this sauce over anything and everything, including this book's loaf and casserole dishes. It is a great flavor enhancer and can be refrigerated for up to 1 week or frozen for up to 3 months. Try freezing in ice cube trays in convenient single-serving portions. When reheating, whisk constantly to blend the ingredients.

> 2 tablespoons butter
> 2 tablespoons flour (I use Wondra®)
> 1 tablespoon Thai fish sauce
> 1 cup fish stock or clam juice

1. In a saucepan over medium heat, whisk together the butter and flour to create a roux, or thick yellow paste.

2. In a measuring cup, gradually whisk the fish sauce into the fish stock or clam juice.

3. Slowly add the fish liquid to the saucepan ¼ cup at a time, whisking constantly and adding more liquid each time the sauce thickens. Repeat until you have used all of the liquid.

4. Allow the sauce to come to a boil, remove from heat, and whisk periodically as it cools to keep it from becoming lumpy.

SAUCE AND GRAVY TIP

I use Gold Medal Wondra® flour, a quick-mixing flour made for sauces and gravies. Because it is very finely milled, it dissolves more quickly than regular flour. The result is a very smooth gravy without lumps.

Saucy Cat®

Saucy Cat® is a registered trademark of mine, but I am giving you the original recipe here. You can sprinkle it dry on food as a flavor enhancer, or add water to make it into a paste or gravy and mix it with or pour it over food. The paste can be spread on old toys to make them interesting again. The great thing about Saucy Cat is that you can store it in a spice jar just like you do your spices. I keep mine in the refrigerator. It will keep for 1 month in the fridge or at least 6 months in the freezer, but it never lasts long in my house. I love to make this during the holidays and give it as a gift. People—and their pets—just love it!

¼ cup freeze-dried liver
1 cup dried fish
½ cup dried beef or chicken
½ cup fish bouillon powder
½ cup parsley flakes
½ cup dried carrots
½ cup celery flakes
½ cup dried tomato flakes (if you can't find flakes, use dried diced tomatoes)
½ cup brewer's yeast (powdered or granular)
1 tablespoon red beet powder

1. Put the dried liver and fish in a blender or food processor and blend into a powder. (I do this on the purée setting.) Set aside.

2. Put the dried beef or chicken in the blender or food processor and blend until the pieces are small enough to go through the holes in a spice jar lid, but are not puréed.

3. Add the dried liver and fish powder and the remaining ingredients to the beef or chicken pieces in the blender or food processor and blend until you are happy with the consistency. I like to keep some small chunks.

7

Fish for the Fish Lover

· ·

ISN'T IT FUNNY HOW DOGS AND CATS HAVE BEEN LABELED? DOGS ARE KNOWN AS MEAT LOVERS, AND CATS ARE NOTORIOUS FOR LOVING FISH, WHEN IN REALITY DOGS ALSO LOVE FISH AND CATS ALSO LOVE MEAT. THE TRUTH IS THAT DOGS ARE OMNIVORES (EATING MEATS AND VEGETABLES) AND CATS ARE CARNIVORES (EATING 90% MEAT).

NEARLY ALL CATS LOVE FISH. THE PROBLEM IS THAT CATS CAN BECOME "TUNA JUNKIES" WHEN THEY ARE OFFERED CANNED TUNA ON A REGULAR BASIS—THEY DON'T WANT TO EAT ANYTHING ELSE. (EVEN VETERINARIANS USE THIS TERM!) IN THIS CHAPTER, YOU WILL FIND A VARIETY OF FISH RECIPES TO MIX UP YOUR CAT'S DIET SO THAT SHE DOESN'T BECOME A TUNA JUNKIE.

Cat Sole

〜 Makes 6 servings 〜

Fillet of sole is a lovely, delicate, white fish. It is mild in flavor and is very easy to cook. I often make this recipe when I am going to cook fillet of sole for the whole family. Both my dogs and my cats truly enjoy it. You can often find fillet of sole flash-frozen and in bulk at grocery superstores. I buy it in bulk, break it up into smaller sizes, double-wrap it, and freeze it so that I can pull out what I need the night before I cook. This recipe cannot be frozen once cooked, but it will keep in the refrigerator for 2 days if stored in an airtight container.

1-pound sole fillet, deboned

½ cup fish stock or water

1 tablespoon olive oil

2 tablespoons chopped fresh parsley or ⅔ teaspoon parsley flakes, plus extra for garnish

¾ cup cooked brown rice

1 tablespoon butter

1½ tablespoons flour

½ cup milk

½ cup grated Parmesan cheese

1 teaspoon salt

½ teaspoon brewer's yeast

2 tablespoons bone meal

1. Preheat the oven to 450 degrees.

2. Put the sole and fish stock or water in a large sauté pan. Bring to a boil; then reduce the heat and simmer until the fish is cooked through, about 5 minutes.

3. Let cool, remove the sole from the pan, and then cut it into small cubes. Reserve the liquid for another use.

4. Add the olive oil to a glass baking dish. Add the cubed sole, parsley, and rice and set aside.

5. Now it's time to make your roux (a French word for a paste). Add the butter to the sauté pan and let it melt slowly over medium-low heat. Gently whisk in the flour, a teaspoon at a time, as the butter melts. Keep whisking until a smooth yellow paste forms.

6. Start slowly whisking in the milk. Add more milk as the sauce thickens. After you have added all the milk, slowly whisk in the Parmesan cheese and salt.

   Note: If you need to add a bit more milk to your sauce, that's okay; sometimes a bit more is needed.

7. Add the brewer's yeast and bone meal to this mixture; it will be thick.

8. Pour the sauce over the fish, sprinkle with additional parsley to garnish, and bake for 10 minutes or until melted and lightly golden brown. Let cool and serve.

All About Roux

There are two types of roux: brown and white. The difference between them is that a brown roux produces a brown sauce and a white roux produces a cream-colored sauce. Making a roux can be a bit tricky, depending on humidity and altitude, but once you have perfected the technique, you will find yourself using it time and time again, whether cooking for your pet or yourself. The basic formula for making a roux is to melt 2 tablespoons butter and then whisk in 2 tablespoons flour. For a brown roux, whisk the flour and butter until a golden brown paste forms. Slowly add beef broth to get the consistency you want for your sauce. For a white roux, slowly whisk in 1 cup milk or chicken broth the minute you have the consistency of paste, before it turns brown. The trick is to do this over medium-low heat, whisking continuously, and add the liquid slowly as the sauce thickens.

Surf and Turf (Fish and Greens)

⸙ Makes 2 servings ⸙

What I mean by "Greens" is a special grass for cats—a grass you can buy from seed or already grown from your pet store, or sometimes at a health food market. It is important to use only grass approved for cats. I suggest oat grass or wheat grass. Make this dish fresh, as it is easy; I don't like to keep this dish for more than 1 or 2 meals.

6-ounce can mackerel in oil
½ cup cooked brown rice
¼ cup cottage cheese
½ cup cut grass

In a large mixing bowl, combine all the ingredients and mix well. Serve fresh.

ALL ABOUT MACKEREL

Mackerel is a fish that is found in the Atlantic Ocean. The mackerel family is comprised of many species. Small mackerels are sold whole, and larger ones are usually sold as fillets. Mackerel can also be purchased salted or smoked. Its flesh is high in fat, and fresh mackerel has a savory flavor. Cooking this fish is limited only by your imagination—it can be prepared in many ways, including sautéing, grilling, frying, baking, and broiling.

Kitty Tostadas

Makes 6 servings

Tex-Mex is one of my favorite comfort foods. This recipe is my nod to a favorite cuisine. This is a great recipe for both cats and dogs. The tuna mixture can be stored in an airtight container in the refrigerator for up to 3 days or in the freezer for 1 month. The tortillas will keep for 2 weeks in the refrigerator or up to 1 month in the freezer if stored in an airtight freezer bag.

4 corn tortillas
2 9-ounce cans dark tuna in oil
½ cup chopped tomatoes
½ cup corn (fresh or canned)
2 tablespoons chopped red bell pepper
¼ cup frozen chopped spinach, thawed and drained
2 tablespoons tomato paste
½ cup grated Cheddar cheese

1. Preheat the oven to 400 degrees. Spray a cookie sheet with nonstick cooking spray.

2. Place the tortillas on the cookie sheet and bake or broil until brown, turning them over midway through. If broiling, this will take about 1 minute per side; if baking, it will take about 2 to 3 minutes per side. Watch closely so that they don't burn.

3. In a sauté pan, sauté the tuna, tomatoes, corn, bell pepper, and spinach for 5 minutes. Add the tomato paste to help thicken and sauté for an additional 5 minutes.

4. Break up the tortillas and sprinkle over each serving to give them a little crunch. Then sprinkle with a little bit of the Cheddar cheese and serve.

Salmon Mousse

Makes 12 servings

I love making this recipe. Not only is it fun, but if you decide to have some cat friends over, this dish is sure to please your friends and their felines. This mousse will keep in the refrigerator for up to 4 days. Do not freeze it.

16-ounce can red salmon, drained
½ cup plain nonfat yogurt
¼ cup hoop cheese (also known as farmer cheese)
1 teaspoon lemon juice
2 packages plain unflavored gelatin
1½ cups chicken stock, divided
1 cup evaporated milk, well chilled

1. Put the salmon, yogurt, cheese, and lemon juice in a blender or food processor and blend until smooth.
2. Soften the gelatin in ½ cup of the (cool) chicken stock. Heat the gelatin–chicken stock mixture gently on the stovetop to liquify it.
3. Add the salmon mixture and the remaining chicken stock to the gelatin on the stovetop.
4. In a large mixing bowl, whip the chilled evaporated milk until stiff. Fold in the salmon mixture.
5. Spray 12 muffin tins with nonstick cooking spray. Pour the salmon mixture into the tins, cover with plastic wrap, and chill in the refrigerator overnight or until firm. Serve.

ALL ABOUT OMEGA-3 FATTY ACIDS

Salmon is packed with omega-3 fatty acids, which can reduce triglycerides. A triglyceride is the form in which most fats exist, both in food and in the body. Omega-3 fatty acids can help reduce the possibility of developing certain cancers and tumors. They also have anti-inflammatory properties and have been shown to reduce the risk of heart attack. Omega-3 fatty acids are also found in menhaden (a member of the herring family) and plants like flax. Some veterinarians prescribe fatty acids for conditions like heart and kidney disease, allergies, arthritis, and some skin problems.

Tasha's Tuna Cakes

I often make these tuna cakes and freeze them. This is a great dinner for a last-minute "What do I feed?" situation. You can take them straight from the freezer and reheat them in a toaster oven or oven. Remember, never serve your cat or dog hot food. These cakes can be stored in the refrigerator for up to 4 days or in the freezer for up to 3 months.

- 2 cups plain dry bread crumbs
- 4 tablespoons plain wheat germ
- 2 9-ounce cans tuna
- 2 eggs
- 1 cup cooked brown rice
- 4 tablespoons chopped fresh parsley, or 1⅓ tablespoons parsley flakes
- 1 tablespoon brewer's yeast
- ½ cup chopped celery
- ½ cup chopped broccoli
- 4 tablespoons melted butter

1. Preheat the oven to 450 degrees. Spray a cookie sheet with nonstick cooking spray.

2. In a medium-sized bowl, mix together the bread crumbs and wheat germ and set aside.

3. Put the tuna, eggs, rice, parsley, brewer's yeast, celery, and broccoli in a blender or food processor and blend for 1 to 2 minutes or until the large chunks are gone; the mixture should not be runny. Pour into a bowl.

4. Form the mixture into 24 to 40 patties that are about 1 inch in diameter and about ½ inch thick. Coat each side well with the bread crumbs–wheat germ mixture.

5. Place the patties on the cookie sheet and drizzle melted butter over each one. Bake for 10 to 15 minutes or until golden brown.

6. Let cool and serve.

Variation: Substitute salmon, mackerel, or sardines for the tuna.

RECIPE ADD-INS: CATNIP AND FISH FLAKES

We all know that cats love fish, but did you know that they also need to have a small amount of greens? If your cat loves catnip, then a fun project is to grow your own. Many pet stores and some all-natural markets sell already-started grow-your-own catnip. You can cut off some fresh catnip and add it to any one of the recipes in this chapter. Not all cats respond to catnip; you will know whether your own cat likes it or not. Test your cat after she reaches 6 months of age.

You can add fish flakes to any of these recipes, too; they are a great source of protein and add a nice flavor. I like to sprinkle them on top of my pets' kibble before baking. I also add them to the tops of my loaves and pasta dishes. You can buy fish flakes at any Asian market; some larger supermarkets stock them in the foreign food section.

Salmon and Sweet Potato Pockets

✹ Makes 8 servings ✹

Be adventurous! This is a really fun recipe. Once you have made all your pockets, you boil them like old-fashioned dumplings. Your cats will love them. I usually freeze 4 pockets together and then defrost them the night before serving. If you want to reheat them, drop them in boiling water for no more than 5 minutes. The pockets will keep for 3 months in the freezer or 4 days in the fridge.

FILLING

6 cups diced salmon

3 cups cubed sweet potatoes, boiled and mashed

1 cup cooked brown rice

1½ cups chopped green beans

1½ cups chopped carrots

1 tablespoon brewer's yeast

¼ cup chopped fresh parsley, or 1⅓ tablespoons parsley flakes

1 tablespoon bone meal

½ teaspoon salt

2 eggs, beaten

In a large mixing bowl, mix together all the ingredients.

CRUST

⅔ cup shortening

3 tablespoons butter

2 cups flour

2 teaspoons baking powder

½ teaspoon salt

2 tablespoons chopped fresh parsley, or 2 teaspoons parsley flakes

3 to 5 cups very cold water

1. Cut the shortening and butter into the flour. Add the baking powder, salt, and parsley and mix until it looks like coarse cornmeal.

2. Add 3 to 5 cups cold water, enough to make the dough the right consistency for rolling. The dough should be smooth, not sticky.

3. Roll out the dough to a thickness of ½ to ¾ inch. Then cut it into 4- to 5-inch squares with a knife. You don't have to be perfect here. If you don't want to roll out your dough, take about 2 tablespoons of dough, flatten it out with floured hands on a floured board, and repeat with the remaining dough.

4. Put 2 tablespoons of the meat mixture inside each square, fold the dough over, and use the back of a fork or your fingers to pinch it closed well.

5. Fill a large stockpot with water and bring it to a boil. Drop the pockets into the boiling water. Cover, turn down the heat, and simmer for 25 minutes. Take the pockets out of the water, let cool, and serve.

Variation: Substitute turkey, chicken, or lamb for the salmon.

CATS' EATING HABITS

Cats have evolved differently than dogs. If you've ever noticed your cat being finicky, one of the reasons is that cats have evolved to eat only fresh food. This is why, when you try to save canned cat food in the refrigerator, your cat may not want to eat it, as it may have acquired odors or flavors from the other foods in your refrigerator. A cat's senses of taste and smell have evolved this way for a good reason: to protect them from getting sick. Do not feed your cat old meat or fish. (A dog is a little less picky and will eat day-old meat if it's offered.)

Did you know that it is also important for a cat to eat every 24 hours? A dog will sometimes skip a meal or two without harm, but a cat has a unique metabolism and in some cases could suffer from hepatic lipidosis (excess fat accumulation in the liver). It is important that cats get an adequate amount of food every day.

8

Bulk Recipes and Budget Meals

· ·

Most of the e-mails I receive about cooking for pets mention how time-consuming and expensive it can be. I'm here to tell you that it doesn't have to be that way. If you set aside a couple of hours for cooking 1 or 2 days a month, you can easily prepare a month's worth of food for your cat. And if you start shopping with recipes in mind, then you can buy turkey, tuna, eggs, fish, and other common ingredients in bulk when you see them on sale. An unopened can of tuna will keep for quite some time. Parmesan cheese can be stored in the freezer for up to 6 months. The same goes for dry pasta—when I see it on sale at the market, I often buy six to ten boxes. If you keep all this in mind, you will find that the cost of cooking for your pet drops dramatically. And learning to do it all in 1 or 2 days a month will make the experience enjoyable for you *and* your cat.

This chapter is filled with recipes that don't require a lot of prep time. Plus, they're all simple to make. Divide these dishes into single-serving portions, seal them in vacuum-sealed food storage bags, and toss them in the freezer for up to 3 months. I like to combine these recipes with a cat's regular kibble in place of canned cat food. These recipes are no-fail, so have fun and be creative!

Sassy Salmon Bake

This layered casserole is fun to make, and cats love its creamy texture. Do not freeze this dish. It will keep in the refrigerator for up to 3 days.

4 small sweet potatoes, peeled and parboiled
16-ounce can salmon, drained
2 tablespoons chopped fresh dill or parsley
1 teaspoon lemon juice
¼ pound thin-sliced lox, cut into small pieces
6 ounces cream cheese, cubed
4 eggs
1¼ cups milk
4 tablespoons fish flakes

1. Preheat the oven to 375 degrees. Spray an 8-inch casserole dish with nonstick cooking spray.

2. Cut the sweet potatoes into ½-inch slices and set aside.

3. In a mixing bowl, mash the salmon.

4. In a separate mixing bowl, combine the dill or parsley, lemon juice, and lox and then add to the salmon.

5. Line the bottom of the casserole dish with a layer of sweet potato slices. Sprinkle half of the cream cheese cubes on top of the potatoes. Spread a layer of the salmon-lox mixture on top of the cream cheese. Add another layer of sweet potatoes, followed by another layer of cream cheese and another layer of the salmon-lox mixture. If you have any sweet potato slices left, put them on top of the lox mixture.

6. In a mixing bowl, beat the eggs and milk. Pour over the layered casserole and sprinkle the fish flakes on top.

7. Bake for 40 minutes or until a knife inserted into the center comes out clean. The top of the casserole should be a bit puffy, like a soufflé. Let cool and serve immediately.

Tuna and Pasta Casserole

⋘ Makes 4 servings ⋙

Believe it or not, many cats love pasta. For this dish, I like to use orzo, the pasta that looks like rice. It's small and easy for cats to chew. I also like to use dark tuna packed in oil, which is a good source of B vitamins. This recipe will keep in the refrigerator for 2 days or in the freezer for 1 month.

> 9-ounce can dark tuna in oil
> ½ cup cooked orzo
> 1 cup fish or vegetable broth
> 2 eggs, beaten
> 1 tablespoon brewer's yeast
> 3 tablespoons chopped fresh parsley, or 1 tablespoon parsley flakes
> 1 tablespoon fish flakes
> ½ cup Parmesan cheese

1. Preheat the oven to 350 degrees. Spray an 8-inch casserole dish with nonstick cooking spray.

2. In a large mixing bowl, combine the tuna, orzo, broth, eggs, brewer's yeast, and parsley.

3. Place the tuna mixture in the casserole dish. Sprinkle the fish flakes and Parmesan cheese on top.

4. Bake for 45 minutes to 1 hour or until a knife inserted into the center comes out clean. Let cool and serve.

Pasta Cooking Tips

Use about 4 quarts of water per pound of pasta you are cooking. Make sure that the water is boiling before you put the pasta in. Add the salt after the water boils, and then add the pasta. Be sure to keep stirring so that the noodles don't stick. If sticking is a problem, add 1 tablespoon of any type of oil. Then be sure to drain the pasta before serving or adding it to a recipe.

Chicken and Greens

〰 Makes 12 servings 〰

As I have said before, cats do need some greens in their diet. Just remember that they need a smaller amount than dogs do. Cats are true carnivores, whereas dogs are omnivores. This recipe will keep in the refrigerator for 1 week and freezes beautifully for up to a month in an airtight container. I like to freeze it in single-serving portions.

> 3-pound roasting chicken, quartered
> 4 cups water
> ½ teaspoon salt
> 2 celery stalks with leaves
> 1 cup finely chopped carrots
> ½ cup chopped fresh parsley, or 2⅔ tablespoons parsley flakes
> ½ cup uncooked barley
> 1 tablespoon lemon juice
> 3 teaspoon brewer's yeast
> 5 ounces frozen chopped spinach, thawed and drained
> 1 cup chopped fresh green beans

1. Place the chicken, water, salt, and leaves from the celery in a large stockpot or slow cooker. (Reserve the celery stalks.) Cover and bring to a boil. Reduce the heat and simmer for 1½ hours or until the chicken is tender.

2. Remove the chicken, strain the broth into a bowl, and chill the broth in the refrigerator until the fat sets on top. Skim off the fat.

3. Remove the fat, skin, and bones from the chicken and discard. Cut the meat into bite-sized pieces and set aside.

4. Return the broth to the pot. Chop the reserved celery stalks and add them to the broth with the carrots, parsley, barley, lemon juice, and brewer's yeast. Cover and simmer for 20 minutes.

5. Add the spinach, green beans, and chicken. Continue cooking for 15 minutes or until the green beans are tender. Let cool and serve.

BARLEY

· ·

Barley is a good source of carbohydrates, which give your pet energy.

Shrimp Rémoulade

〽 Makes 6 to 8 servings 〽

This no-fail recipe is fun and easy to make, and every cat loves it. The dish is high in protein and vitamins. Do *not* freeze it. It will keep for up to 3 days in the refrigerator.

2 hard-cooked eggs, mashed

1 teaspoon anchovy paste

½ cup cottage cheese

1 teaspoon brewer's yeast

1 pound boiled shrimp, cleaned, with tails removed

3 tablespoons chopped fresh parsley, or 1 tablespoon parsley flakes

1. In a blender, purée the eggs, anchovy paste, cottage cheese, and brewer's yeast to make the rémoulade sauce.

2. Chop the shrimp into bite-sized pieces.

3. Pour the rémoulade sauce over the shrimp, sprinkle with parsley, and serve.

ALL ABOUT SHRIMP

Shrimp come in seven sizes: colossal, jumbo, extra-large, large, medium, small, and mini or bay shrimp. When buying shrimp, look for raw shrimp that are firm, moist, and translucent. They should smell like the sea, not like ammonia. If you have to deshell and devein your shrimp, slice down the back and then remove the shell, tail, and inner intestine. (The intestine looks like a little brown string.) Wash the shrimp thoroughly and dry them with a paper towel. If you're boiling your shrimp, boil them until they are pink all the way through. The average size shrimp takes about 10 minutes to cook.

Thai Seafood Dinner

Thai fish sauce is one of my favorite ingredients—I always keep it in the pantry. It adds a great intense flavor. Just remember that it can be high in sodium, so a little goes a long way. This recipe is so easy that on one of the days you set aside for cooking, you could make this dinner and a loaf recipe and have a month's worth of cat food in your freezer. This dish will keep for 2 days in the refrigerator or 1 month in the freezer.

6½-ounce can chopped clams

2-ounce can anchovies

2 tablespoons brewer's yeast

2 tablespoons Thai fish sauce

½ cup cooked brown rice

2 tablespoons chopped fresh parsley, or 2 teaspoons parsley flakes

1. In a blender or food processor, blend the clams, anchovies, brewer's yeast, and fish sauce.

2. In a saucepan over medium heat, combine the fish mixture with the brown rice and parsley. Cook for 10 minutes or until heated through. Let cool and serve.

RICE TIP

Try cooking your rice in beef or chicken broth—doing so adds a lot of flavor. It will also help entice your cat to eat, especially if she is feeling under the weather. Remember, pets are scent driven!

Purrfect Pasta

I like to use a ring mold for this recipe; it looks cool and is fun to use. This dish freezes well for up to 3 months and will keep in the refrigerator for 3 days.

3 cups cubed chicken

2 cups shredded carrots

2 cups shredded apples

2 cups peas

2 cups chopped green beans

1 cup canned plain pumpkin

2 cups cooked pasta, any shape (I use baby elbows)

5 tablespoons plain wheat germ

¼ cup chopped fresh parsley, or 1⅓ tablespoons parsley flakes

1 cup shredded cheese, any type (I use Monterey Jack cheese)

1 tablespoon brewer's yeast

2 eggs, beaten

½ cup Parmesan cheese

1. Preheat the oven to 350 degrees. Spray a ring mold with nonstick cooking spray.

2. In a large mixing bowl, mix together everything except the eggs and Parmesan cheese.

3. Pour the mixture into the ring mold. Pour the beaten eggs over the mixture and sprinkle the Parmesan cheese on top.

4. Bake for 1 hour or until the mold is well set and a knife inserted into the center comes out clean. Let cool and serve.

Whole Roaster Chicken for a Big Meal

At the end of the day, grocery stores often put the precooked rotisserie chickens on special. I buy them and either use them immediately or freeze them for later. They are inexpensive, and they can be huge timesavers, as in this recipe. This dish will keep for 3 days in the refrigerator and up to 3 months in the freezer.

1 precooked rotisserie roasted chicken
9-ounce can dark tuna in oil
1 cup cooked brown rice
1 cup frozen chopped spinach, thawed and drained
2 eggs, beaten
½ cup chopped fresh parsley, or 1⅓ tablespoons parsley flakes
4 tablespoons plain wheat germ
3 tablespoons brewer's yeast
¼ cup chopped carrots

1. Preheat the oven to 350 degrees. Spray a casserole dish with nonstick cooking spray.

2. Remove the skin and bones from the chicken. Shred or chop the chicken, whichever you prefer—just make sure you end up with bite-sized pieces.

3. In a large mixing bowl, combine the chicken, tuna, rice, spinach, eggs, parsley, wheat germ, brewer's yeast, and carrots.

4. Spread the mixture in the casserole dish. Bake for 1 hour or until golden brown; a knife inserted in the center should come out clean. Let cool and serve.

Fancy Fish Balls

Makes 10 servings

Last year, for a magazine photo shoot, they requested that I make my fancy fish cakes. The problem was that I had only 24 hours' notice to cook eight recipes for the shoot *and* get myself ready. So I came up with this easy alternative. The fish balls looked great, and no one even noticed I hadn't made fish cakes. In one of the photos, there were six cats sitting around a big table. The large cat, Mr. Love, could not stop at just one fish ball. He loved them! Now I'm sharing this wonderful recipe with you and your pet. You can refrigerate these fish balls for 3 days or freeze them for 2 months.

9-ounce can dark tuna in oil, drained

2 ounces cooked herring, skin removed

6 baby carrots, boiled until tender and then mashed

1 egg, beaten

3 tablespoons grated Parmesan cheese

2 tablespoons tomato paste

2 teaspoons brewer's yeast

¼ teaspoon catnip

2 tablespoons plain dry bread crumbs

2 tablespoons rolled oats

2 tablespoons plain wheat germ

1. Preheat the oven to 350 degrees. Spray a cookie sheet with nonstick cooking spray.

2. In a mixing bowl, combine the tuna, herring, carrots, egg, Parmesan cheese, tomato paste, brewer's yeast, and catnip and mix well.

3. In another bowl, mix together the bread crumbs, rolled oats, and wheat germ.

4. Form the fish mixture into 1-inch balls, and then roll them in the bread crumb mixture until coated well.

5. Place the balls 1 inch apart on the cookie sheet and bake for 15 to 20 minutes or until golden brown and firm. A toothpick inserted into the balls should come out clean.

6. Let cool on wire racks and serve.

BREWER'S YEAST

Brewer's yeast is an excellent source of essential fatty acids and B-complex vitamins for a glossy coat and a stable nervous system.

Index